UNREADY TO LEAD
HOW AMERICA'S LEADERS ARE BUILT

OLUWABIYI ADEYEMO

UNREADY TO LEAD: How America's Leaders Are Built

Copyright © 2025 by Oluwabiyi Adeyemo

All rights reserved. No part of this book may be reproduced, stored in a retrieval system, or transmitted in any form or by any means including electronic, mechanical, photocopying, or recording without written permission from the publisher, except for brief quotations used in reviews or critical articles.

Published in the United States of America
ISBN: 978-8-9936477-2-2
Published by
The SozoRock Foundation
Albany, New York

This work opens the Leadership Series and examines how leaders rise in the United States without the preparation their roles demand and how unreadiness affects teams, institutions, and the nation.

Printed in the United States of America

Many people contributed to the experiences that shaped the lessons in these pages. Some opened doors. Others presented challenges. Each one sharpened my understanding of what readiness really means.

I am grateful to the leaders who invited me into their boardrooms, the public officials who trusted my guidance, and the individuals who chose integrity in moments most people overlook. Their actions, both helpful and difficult, revealed the patterns that later became the insights shared here.

I also appreciate those who encouraged my thinking when the work felt heavy. Their support made clarity possible.

Above all, I thank God for strength, direction, and the opportunity to turn personal experience into principles others can use.

CONTENTS

LEADERSHIP SERIES NOTE 7

ONE: THE QUIET COLLAPSE 10
The Forum That Revealed a Nation's Blind Spot 15
The Passport That Never Was 19
The Invisible Decay of Readiness 22
The Cost of Assumption 27
The Crisis of Competence 35
Power Without Readiness 42

TWO: THE MISSING LINK AT THE SUMMIT 52
The Poverty Plate 58
Locked on the Tarmac 63
The Venture That Would Not Stand 69
Learning Beside Real Decisions 76
Sponsorship That Costs Something 78
Closing the Gap at the Summit 82

THREE: PREPARED BY HUSTLE, PAID BY TRUST 86
Persuasion — Alignment in Action 102
Negotiation — Protecting Value Without Burning Bridges 114
The Language of Gesture 119
The Silent Killers of Negotiation 124
Resilience in the Storm 131

The Imperative	142
Mentorship Multiplies Leadership	145
When Price Overshadows Value	155
The Value Guardrails	158
Finding the Sweet Spot	159
The Flexibility Matrix	161
The Salesman in the Corner Office	162
The Law of Persuasion	164
ABOUT THE AUTHOR	**167**

LEADERSHIP SERIES NOTE

Leadership rises or falls on preparation. Many people accept responsibility before they are ready for the weight it carries. The expectations arrive immediately. The habits needed to meet those expectations often arrive slowly. You can see the effects in companies, schools, hospitals, and public institutions. Progress slows. Confidence weakens. Teams work harder than necessary, and leaders feel pressure they were never trained to handle.

The purpose of this series is to explain why unreadiness has become so common and how to correct it with practical steps. Readiness is not personality or talent. It is the product of daily choices. People become effective when they learn to think with clarity, act with discipline, and accept responsibility without waiting for a title. When these qualities are missing, even highly skilled individuals struggle. When these qualities are present, ordinary people achieve remarkable results.

This book focuses on the core problem. It examines the moments when unreadiness becomes visible and the quiet patterns that create it. It also looks at the ways organizations often promote people faster than they prepare them. The goal is simple. You cannot strengthen leadership until you understand where it breaks down.

A future book in this series will focus on solutions. It will outline the systems and practices that build capable leaders. It will show how to strengthen judgment, decision making, confidence, and consistency. It will also offer practical steps for institutions that want to raise standards while creating room for growth.

The larger purpose of this work is to help individuals, teams, and communities. A strong nation depends on leaders who are prepared for the responsibilities they accept. When people are ready, they build trust, create momentum, and set an example that others can follow.

These pages are written to help you recognize the cost of unreadiness and to understand the advantage of preparing long before the responsibility arrives.

ONE

THE QUIET COLLAPSE

No alarm was raised. No memo marked the change. No headline told anyone to take notice. What unfolded was a quiet fading of confidence behind daily routines. Meetings ran longer but produced little. Emails grew more frequent while decisions became fewer. Leaders spoke with conviction in public and hesitated in private. It was not scandal that weakened them. It was something harder to see—unreadiness growing quietly.

I felt it before I could describe it. After each boardroom meeting I knew the hardest work was still waiting. Everyone had talked at length, but no one had taken charge of the next step. Patterns began to appear. The talk about progress was loud, the practice of progress quiet. Hours were busy, calendars packed, yet the results never matched the energy spent.

This quiet decline showed up in places that should have been ready. Long-established schools were shaken by one unexpected event. Accredited hospitals stumbled when procedures met human fear. Well-known companies with polished plans found no alignment in the teams that had to deliver. Local governments with strong public support discovered that enthusiasm cannot replace policy and goodwill does not balance an account.

The collapse did not arrive as disorder. It arrived as absence: a missing process where one should have been, a missing successor who was never trained, a missing decision when time ran out. Unreadiness rarely begins with crisis; it begins with habit. It starts when a team assumes someone else will prepare and when leaders mistake visibility for competence and titles for judgment.

I saw my own reflection in it. Early in my career I thought energy could replace structure and that talent alone could carry the load meant for systems. I kept telling myself we would figure it out when we arrived. When we finally did, there was nothing firm beneath us. Deadlines slipped, not from carelessness but from untested handoffs. Clients grew impatient, not because they wanted more, but because we had promised clarity and delivered motion. That was the day I learned the first rule of readiness: it never happens by accident; it must be built intentionally.

When a team struggles, the signs are always there. An agenda without names beside the tasks. A plan that never defines what "ready" means. A leader confident on stage but hesitant when the room is empty. These are not signs of incompetence but of a culture that sees preparation as optional. When preparation becomes optional, crisis becomes certain.

I saw the cost in people. Teachers who cared deeply but had never practiced a simple emergency plan. Nurses who knew every protocol yet had never led a briefing under pressure. Managers who could present slides but could not align their peers. Young officials who wanted to serve their cities but had never learned how to turn intent into policy or budget. Motivation was there. Method was missing.

Unreadiness has a sound. It is the sound of careful voices asking for one more meeting, of rooms that choose comfort over commitment, of leaders who promise to follow up and let time close the door. By the time the story reaches the news, the real collapse has already happened in smaller rooms no one remembers.

I once left a long meeting of public and private leaders. Everyone agreed the issue was urgent. Everyone praised the presentation. Everyone thanked one another for their insights. Yet no one claimed the first action that would reach the real world by morning. In the elevator I wrote a note that I have never forgotten: Urgency without ownership is theater.

This is how public expectation changes. At first people are surprised when leaders hesitate. Then they get used to it. Soon they expect it. The real danger is not the loss of trust in institutions but the quiet loss of belief that anyone is ready at all. When that belief fades, people ask for less, teams reach for less, and talent looks for shortcuts. In that space, noise takes over. Influencers replace experts, slogans replace plans, and anger replaces patience—because readiness was ignored for too long.

I did not learn this from reports. I learned it by watching what was missing in rooms where I worked and rooms I only observed. I saw confident people face moments that needed more than confidence, bright minds falter when timing mattered more than analysis, and good people tire because their system forced them to improvise each week. The answer was not new language but old discipline made daily again.

When I teach readiness, I start with three questions. What does "ready" look like for this decision? Who owns it by name? When will the next irreversible act happen? These questions are not dramatic and they need no slide. They push a team from talk to action, from meeting to commitment, from hope to plan. Most of all, they show whether a culture values preparation or only performs it when someone is watching.

The quiet collapse can be reversed. The work is simple but not glamorous. It is the steady practice of small habits until they become instinct. It is arriving before the room fills, writing a one-page definition of "done" for every key task, training a deputy who can step in tomorrow instead of next year, rehearsing choices before crisis demands them, and measuring leaders not only by results but by what continues in their absence.

I have seen organizations make this change. The energy in the room shifts. People stop speaking in general terms. Deadlines become promises. Messages shorten because intent is shared. Younger staff stand taller because responsibility is spread, not guarded. Senior leaders breathe easier because they trust the chain beneath them. The public does not see these shifts right away, but they feel them when things start working again.

Readiness is not dramatic. It is a habit repeated until it becomes culture. It reminds every team that order matters, timing matters, and promises must turn into action. It removes the illusion that talk is the same as execution and replaces hope with practice that makes progress real.

I began with silence because that is where collapse hides. The first duty of a leader is to notice what the room no longer says. When talk becomes polite, ask harder questions. When meetings run long, name owners and times. When a plan looks impressive, find the step that reaches a customer, a classroom, a clinic, or a street. Leadership lives in that step, and readiness is proven there.

One idea has guided me since I learned to see this quiet decline. Progress begins the moment you name what is missing and take ownership of the next step that cannot be undone.

The Forum That Revealed a Nation's Blind Spot

In 2007, I organized a leadership forum that reshaped my understanding of readiness. What began as a small event had grown into one of the largest cross-sector gatherings of emerging leaders. That year, attendance passed twenty thousand. The scale had outgrown a single venue, so we divided the sessions. On one day, I spoke to one group myself; on the next, the rest met with a guest—usually a Fortune 100 executive or a senior public official among the top five in national leadership.

The theme that year was Synergy Between Skill and Character. I chose it because leadership collapses when either is missing. I had seen smart people lose credibility when character gave way under pressure and good people fail because skill alone could not carry responsibility. The forum was not a speaking showcase; it was a proving ground where readiness—or its absence—was visible in real time.

I first met the guest speaker the year before, in 2006, when he was Attorney General of a state in an African nation. Earlier, he had served at the International Criminal Court in The Hague, assisting a senior judge. His path from that courtroom to public service showed precision, principle, and persistence. By the time we met, he was already known for discipline and integrity. In the years ahead, he would become Vice President and serve two full terms—eight years that tested his beliefs about leadership. His rise from Attorney General to Vice President represented the kind of steady growth seen in societies that prepare leaders deliberately.

We met during an international event. After the session he walked with my team toward the parking area. As I sat in the car, he leaned to the window and said quietly, "Let's exchange numbers for future purposes." It was a simple moment but one I never forgot. It showed humility, curiosity, and foresight—

qualities that often fade as people rise in influence. We stayed in touch, and when the time came to plan the next forum, I invited him to speak.

He arrived an hour early. The event was set for eight, but by seven he was there—calm, courteous, and prepared. That simple act said more about leadership than any keynote could. Punctuality may seem small, yet it reveals culture. It shows respect for others' time and readiness for responsibility. In leadership, punctuality is not about the clock; it is about the standard it sets. It tells every team that discipline must come before decision.

When he took the stage, his words were calm and clear. There was no showmanship. Every sentence carried weight because it came from experience. Then he shared a story I have never forgotten.

A man once received an opportunity to travel abroad. His visa application was approved, and everything moved smoothly until the embassy asked for his passport the day before his appointment. He did not have one. He had never applied. The opportunity ended with that question. It was not ability that failed him. It was unreadiness.

The hall went silent. Everyone understood the meaning. It was not a story about travel; it was about leadership. It showed how people and institutions lose ground, not from lack of talent but from failing to prepare for tomorrow's demands. Unreadiness is rarely personal; it is cultural.

The story was not about paperwork. It was about culture. It showed the risk of living without looking ahead. The same truth applies to leadership. Opportunities rarely give notice. They appear suddenly and they do not wait. Those who prepare in advance take them; those who delay lose both the chance and the trust that comes with it.

That day I understood that preparation is not formality; it is foundation. An unready passport mirrors an unready organization. Across many institutions, vacancies open before successors are trained, and decisions stall because no one rehearsed the process ahead of time. When preparation is postponed, opportunity collapses before it starts.

The image of that forgotten passport has stayed with me because unreadiness makes no sound. It shows itself through silence—missed meetings, unanswered calls, delayed projects, and leaders who look confident until responsibility arrives.

The theme proved prophetic. Synergy Between Skill and Character was more than a topic; it was the missing ingredient in many systems. Skill without character weakens trust. Character without skill slows progress. Both must stand together, or readiness collapses.

From that moment, I began to notice readiness everywhere—or its absence. It showed in who arrived early, how teams rehearsed, and how calmly institutions faced change. Readiness was never about money or eloquence; it was about discipline and consistency.

That morning, the Attorney General's quiet punctuality taught me what no lecture could: leadership is proven before the spotlight turns on.

The Passport That Never Was

After the forum, I kept thinking about the story he told on stage. It was simple but deeply revealing. A man had been invited to travel abroad. His visa was approved, his papers complete, his sponsor ready to pay the cost. Then the embassy asked for his passport. He had never applied. The chance disappeared overnight.

It was not a story about travel. It was a story about readiness. It showed that opportunity seldom gives notice and that success belongs to those who prepare before they are called. That morning I understood that unreadiness is rarely weakness; it is waiting. It appears when preparation begins only after the moment of demand.

The lesson stayed with me through every leadership setting I encountered. The missing passport became a symbol of missing structure and missing systems. It showed what happens when organizations move with energy but without method. In schools, it becomes the lack of a crisis plan. In companies, it is the absence of succession. In government, it is the habit of improvising instead of planning ahead.

Unreadiness often looks calm until it is tested. Emails are sent, meetings held, reports written. But when pressure comes, no one knows who decides, who speaks, or what to do next. It is the quiet before failure—the slow erosion that turns movement into standstill.

That story stayed with me because it reminded me of a truth every leader must learn. Preparation is not a task; it is a culture. You cannot borrow it when needed, and you cannot invent it when the spotlight turns on. Preparation builds confidence long before the opportunity appears.

Through the years I saw the same pattern repeat. Leaders assumed they would have time to prepare when opportunity arrived. They rarely did. One project failed because a key person was untrained. Another partnership collapsed because communication was never tested. Each loss looked sudden, yet every one of them was predictable.

Unreadiness makes no noise. It hides behind polite meetings and phrases like, "We'll cross that bridge when we get there." It waits quietly until the bridge gives way, and by then it is too late to rebuild.

The passport story revealed something deeper about people. Many capable men and women confuse talent with timing. They believe ability alone opens doors. But doors open only for those prepared to walk through them. Talent attracts opportunity; readiness decides whether it lasts.

Preparation, I learned, is not paperwork. It is the steady alignment of competence, character, and consistency. It turns potential into trust and becomes the unseen foundation of credibility.

Unreadiness reveals itself through what is missing—the backup that isn't there, the order that never forms, the successor who has not been trained. It is the missing passport, the missing leader, the missing next in line. That is how systems fail quietly while everyone assumes all is well.

That is why readiness must be a discipline. It cannot be inherited, delegated, or borrowed. It must be built every day until it becomes instinct. When the moment comes—and it always does—it will not wait.

That year's theme, Synergy Between Skill and Character, proved itself in that story. Skill without preparation breaks under pressure. Character without preparation hesitates in uncertainty. Real readiness appears only when both stand firm together.

That single image—a man standing before an embassy window, opportunity within reach, unreadiness beside him—has remained my lifelong reminder. Leadership rarely fails from lack of ability; it fails when people stop preparing for tomorrow.

The Invisible Decay of Readiness

Unreadiness does not arrive with alarms. It grows quietly, layer by layer, beneath the surface of progress. At first it is hard to notice. It hides behind competence, confidence, and polished presentations. It waits until responsibility becomes real. Then it appears.

The collapse of readiness is rarely dramatic. There is no explosion, no public scandal, no single decision to blame. It is a steady decay that begins when small disciplines are ignored and continues until whole systems lose the capacity to respond. It is happening in schools, hospitals, city offices, and corporate suites, and it is easy to miss because it begins in silence.

I once sat in a boardroom after a public setback. The executives spoke fluently, used expert jargon, and analyzed the event with skill. As the meeting stretched on, no one made a clear decision. No next step was named. The room was full of intellect and short on ownership. That was the real collapse. Readiness had turned into commentary. They did not need new skills. They needed new habits.

Unreadiness begins this way. People substitute talk for traction, plans for practice, optimism for structure. Because the early stages are quiet, people mistake calm for control.

I saw the same quiet decay in a school district crisis. It began with a small misunderstanding, one student's frustration amplified online. Within hours, outrage spread across the community. The administrators were skilled and dedicated, yet they were caught off guard. They issued conflicting statements that sounded responsible but deepened confusion. Meetings multiplied, emotions rose, and within days trust collapsed. It took years to rebuild what unreadiness ruined in a week.

When I looked back, five gaps were clear. No one anticipated a crisis. No one took ownership. Calm was lost early. Empathy was absent from the public response. After the storm passed, no one debriefed to prevent the next one. This pattern repeats in many places. The issue is not intelligence. It is the habit of skipping the daily disciplines that build readiness before a crisis.

Unreadiness inside an organization behaves like rust. It begins at the edges with a missed meeting, a delayed response, a vague instruction, and spreads inward until even the core becomes fragile. By the time the damage is visible, repair costs far more than prevention.

I remember a major financial institution. The CEO was decisive, confident, and aligned. One level below her, unreadiness had taken root. The executive director who stalled the project was not incompetent. He was trapped by ego, and ego is an early symptom of unreadiness. When people protect territory more than team, fear is hiding behind authority.

When I met him on the stairwell, I had a choice. I could mirror his frustration or model readiness. I chose to model readiness. I reframed the issue in his terms, outcomes, timelines, and institutional benefit. Resistance shifted to collaboration. Ego gave way to alignment. Momentum returned. It also revealed a truth I have seen many times. Unreadiness in the middle weakens readiness at the top.

That is the silent decay of execution. People still care, yet the fear of loss outweighs the discipline of alignment. Each level waits for someone else to move first.

Unreadiness also lives in language. It sounds like, "Let's wait and see." It sounds like, "We have always done it this way." It hides behind, "It is probably fine." Each time those phrases are spoken, the muscles of readiness weaken.

The psychology of unreadiness is simple and dangerous. People avoid preparation not because they are lazy, but because preparation requires confrontation. It forces you to face uncertainty, test assumptions, and make decisions that expose judgment. Many avoid that discomfort. They choose the illusion of stability over real responsibility. Leadership does the opposite. It begins where comfort ends.

Unreadiness is not only personal, it is contagious. A late leader teaches lateness. A vague manager teaches vagueness. A reactive culture trains people to wait for problems instead of preventing them. Over time, people stop believing readiness matters. That is how decay becomes culture.

You can see it in metrics. Productivity looks stable while initiative declines. Deadlines are met while creativity fades. The numbers look fine until a disruption exposes how brittle the system is. Then everyone scrambles and wonders how strength disappeared.

It disappeared because daily disciplines were lost. Readiness is built like health, one small decision at a time. Decay works like illness, ignored symptoms, missed checkups, postponed treatments.

The equation is simple.
Readiness = Clarity + Discipline + Anticipation.
Decay = Comfort + Delay + Excuse.

Every leader lives between these two formulas. Every decision either strengthens readiness or speeds decay.

Look closely and unreadiness has a sound, a rhythm, and a feeling. You hear it in meetings that end without ownership, see it in reports without conclusions, and feel it in teams that are busy but not aligned. It is the quiet erosion of momentum that looks like productivity.

Unreadiness looks stable until it is tested. The system appears orderly. The documents are in folders. The titles sound impressive. The first moment of pressure exposes everything. Pressure does not create weakness. It reveals it.

In every system that thrives, three traits are always visible, anticipation, accountability, and adaptability. Anticipation keeps people looking ahead. Accountability keeps people from hiding behind hierarchy. Adaptability turns lessons into structure. Remove one of these and decay begins.

Leaders ask me, "How do you know if a team is ready?" I tell them, "Stress it before reality does." Readiness grows in practice, not theory. Run simulations. Ask hard questions. Create small tests that reveal how people think when they are uncertain. When the real test comes, there is no rehearsal.

Unreadiness does not always look like crisis. Sometimes it looks like calm. It looks like a team that smiles but avoids responsibility. It looks like a department that performs well alone but resists collaboration. It looks like a leader who listens politely but does not follow up. Many symptoms of unreadiness hide behind the appearance of control.

The collapse of readiness is not only a leadership failure. It is a cultural failure. Institutions decay not because of one weak link but because readiness stopped being everyone's job. The answer is not punishment. It is clarity. Everyone must know what readiness means for them, how it is measured, and why it matters.

Readiness begins in silence as well. It begins in the early hours before the day starts, when a leader reviews priorities and asks, "If this day changes, am I ready?" That question separates those who react from those who lead.

Unreadiness will test leaders at every level. The choice is to wait for the test or prepare for it. Every delay in preparation is an invitation to collapse.

When collapse comes, it is not loud. It is quiet, efficient, and complete.

That is the invisible decay of readiness.

The Cost of Assumption

Assumption is one of the most expensive liabilities in leadership. It rarely shows up in reports and rarely invites concern when an operation appears calm. It slips into decisions through untested confidence, unconfirmed commitments, and systems held together by habit instead of discipline. Over time, those assumptions settle into routine, and that routine becomes the hidden structure that lifts a team or quietly weakens it.

Readiness does not fail with a dramatic collapse. It fails the moment a leader assumes preparation where preparation has not been proven. Meetings are held, plans are drafted, responsibilities are assigned, and everyone walks away with the sense that the work is complete. Yet nothing has been tested under real pressure. The plan looks strong on paper while the structure beneath it is empty.

I have watched this pattern repeat itself across many industries. It begins with a plan that no one validates and ends with a crisis that surprises no one who looks closely. I remember listening to a project leader who spoke confidently about a launch and assured everyone that every department was aligned. A few weeks later, the first delay surfaced. A vendor missed a deadline, and the team discovered that no one had confirmed a backup supplier. The scramble began. Costs increased. Confidence faded. No one had acted irresponsibly. They had simply acted on assumptions.

The same principle governs national planning. Policy failure does not appear out of nowhere. It grows from untested readiness. Budgets are drafted without scenario planning. Disaster plans ignore supply chain weaknesses. Agencies rely on single points of expertise with no succession in place. Failure in these situations is not accidental. It follows a predictable path created through long periods of assumption.

I learned this lesson early in my own work. As my responsibilities expanded, the accuracy of preparation began to determine the results of events, negotiations, and partnerships. During a major conference, the sound system failed minutes before a live broadcast. The generator operator had left for lunch because he was convinced his work was complete. No one had been assigned to support him. The delay felt longer than it was, and the tension in the room stayed with me. I realized that assumption often feels efficient until it destroys credibility.

The most damaging assumptions are not about logistics or timelines. They are about people. Leaders assume that instructions were understood. They assume that enthusiasm will translate into follow-through. They assume that silence means agreement. These are the assumptions that weaken culture one interaction at a time.

I once worked with a senior executive who avoided checking details because he believed that trust alone would inspire excellence. It sounded admirable. It felt supportive. Yet a series of preventable errors grew into a public setback. When I asked him what happened, he said the sentence I have heard in many boardrooms. "I thought they had it covered." That sentence has ended more careers and projects than any scandal ever could.

The answer is not suspicion. The answer is verification. The most effective leaders I have studied were not driven by doubt. They were driven by clarity. They trusted their teams, and they confirmed their progress. They understood that confidence without confirmation becomes negligence disguised as optimism.

One global banking executive demonstrated this principle better than any leadership seminar. Before every major rollout, he arrived an hour early and walked the floors quietly. He asked simple questions. "Who handles the contingency plan?" "When was the last test completed?" "What is the response if the network stops?" His tone was calm. He was not policing his team. He was protecting the mission. Results improved because people knew their leader cared enough to see the work for himself.

When I asked why he made the visits personally, he gave an answer I have repeated to leaders around the world. "People perform to the level that leadership checks, not the level it assumes." That sentence has guided me through every project I have led. It captures the essence of readiness. Accountability is created through verification.

Assumption also kills learning. Once people believe a system works simply because it has worked before, they stop examining it. Routines continue without thought. No one asks whether the process still fits the moment. When feedback stops, improvement stops. Innovation does not disappear suddenly. It fades quietly under the weight of assumption. Meetings continue. Activity continues. But discovery is gone.

Over time, organizations experience what I call competence fatigue. It appears slowly. People sound informed, yet the work yields less. Conversations grow longer, analysis grows heavier, and progress becomes thin. Confidence remains strong, but results flatten. The problem is not effort. The problem is an inability to see the erosion taking place.

Every high-performing leader I have coached faced this same temptation. They refused to let familiarity replace curiosity. They continued to ask questions others ignored. They refused to accept easy explanations. Curiosity, not authority, protects a team from decline. When a leader stops asking questions, the decline has already begun.

This is why readiness cannot be accidental. It cannot depend on memory, personality, or good intentions. It must be built into structure. It requires documented steps, tested contingencies, and people who know not only their responsibilities but also who steps in when they cannot. Any system that depends on perfect conditions is already broken. It simply has not been tested yet.

Leaders who understand readiness are easy to recognize. Their meetings begin with confirmation. Their questions are specific. "What happens if this fails?" "Who has the authority to respond?" "How will we know we are drifting off course?" These are not questions born from fear. They are signs of discipline.

Unreadiness always hides in the same sentence. "We thought it was handled." I have heard those words in corporate reviews, in city meetings, and in national briefings. Each time that sentence points to one issue. Someone assumed instead of verifying.

The remedy starts with humility. No system is flawless, and no leader sees everything. Strength is not the ability to pretend otherwise. Strength is the willingness to reveal uncertainty early enough to correct it. Humility keeps leaders alert before a situation forces them to react.

Readiness is not about adding more work. It is about better thinking. It demands clarity about what can go wrong and a firm grasp on what must go right. When that clarity exists, trust grows naturally. It does not need to be promoted. People see competence at work.

To test readiness, I often ask three questions that expose assumption immediately.

Who makes the first decision in an emergency?
Who steps in if that person cannot act?
How will everyone else be informed?

If the answers are not immediate, unreadiness is already present.

Assumption may feel faster in the moment. It saves minutes now and costs months later. Real efficiency comes from removing surprises. A few minutes spent confirming today prevent long stretches of repair tomorrow.

I learned this again while advising a large organization on a major partnership. The opportunity was strong and every team felt aligned. Yet in the final week, an overlooked compliance clause halted the entire process. Each group assumed the other had reviewed it. Weeks of preparation froze because of a single question no one had asked. "Who verified this?" That question separates confident talk from competent leadership.

Assumption also drains another resource. It steals the time leaders need for improvement. When energy is spent fixing preventable issues, innovation slows. Readiness protects time as much as it protects trust.

The strongest organizations operate with a simple rhythm. They check, they confirm, and they act. They do not confuse verification with doubt. They view it as respect for the mission. Their people remain clear. Their systems remain steady. Their leaders remain calm when pressure rises.

In the end, readiness is not measured by how many plans exist. It is measured by how well a team moves when those plans are tested. The absence of panic shows the presence of preparation.

The cost of assumption reaches beyond money. It affects confidence in leadership. It weakens the quiet belief that someone is paying attention. When that belief fades, even talented teams lose momentum. People stop stretching because they no longer feel seen.

Leadership at its highest level requires a different discipline. It calls for steady vigilance and preparation that feels natural. The finest leaders treat readiness as instinct rather than reaction.

They remove assumption before it becomes habit. They replace uncertainty with structure and routine with resilience.

Every crisis I have examined, from boardrooms to national institutions, traces back to one early decision. Somewhere a leader believed readiness could be assumed. Once that belief settles in, it spreads quietly until reality exposes the weakness.

The choice in front of every leader is clear. Build a culture that confirms or continue a culture that assumes. Shape a team that prepares or maintain one that reacts. Seek the truth before a crisis or wait until a crisis reveals it.

When readiness becomes culture, pressure does not create panic. It reveals strength. People stay calm. Decisions hold. Credibility deepens.

But when assumption continues unchallenged, another shift begins. The surface still looks polished, but capability weakens inside. Confidence stays loud, but competence starts to thin. That quiet erosion sets the stage for the next level of failure. Leaders appear prepared, yet the foundation beneath them has already begun to give way.

That is the crisis of competence, and it is where we now turn.

The Crisis of Competence

I have learned through years of coaching leaders that competence is not talent. It is the steady result of training reinforced through disciplined habits. Yet I watched a troubling pattern emerging across many fields. People were rising faster than they were developing. Titles advanced, but maturity did not. Decisions increased, yet judgment weakened. Intelligence was not the issue. They had never been trained to think, decide, and sustain focus at the speed their responsibilities required.

I noticed this long before it became a national concern. I saw it in boardrooms where confusion looked like confidence. I saw it in classrooms where activity replaced mastery. I saw it in community meetings where long discussions produced no clear direction. The appearance of competence replaced the practice of competence. Reports were written but never reviewed. Meetings opened on time but ended without decisions. Teams worked hard but rarely aligned.

The decline of competence seldom arrives with drama. It starts in subtle moments. A leader hesitates when clarity is needed. Meetings replace difficult conversations. A long email trail avoids accountability. I once attended a two-hour review where every department explained why no progress had been made. No one was lying. They were simply exhausted. Their habits had shifted from readiness to reaction.

This shift has the same effect everywhere. Leaders confuse motion for progress. They remain busy because they fear stopping. They measure output through effort rather than results. I learned early that the difference between competence and collapse is not intelligence. It is clarity under pressure. Without that clarity, even the most gifted leader eventually falls behind.

A woman appointed to lead a national initiative taught me this lesson again. On paper, she was ideal. Trusted. Intelligent. Highly regarded. Yet within weeks she felt overwhelmed. Each decision required another meeting. Each policy stalled. She had a room full of advisors but felt isolated. Her knowledge was strong, but her structure was weak. She worked constantly, yet little moved forward.

One afternoon, after a difficult meeting, she stood near the window sorting her notes. Her hands trembled as she tried to organize her thoughts. She had spent an entire day listening, yet nothing had advanced. Later, I asked to see her calendar. It was packed from morning to evening with no space to think. We removed a third of her obligations. We created thinking time. We defined three daily priorities. The change was immediate. Her decisions sharpened. Her energy returned. Her team regained trust. She did not improve through motivation. She improved through order. Competence grows in structure.

I have seen this in every industry. When leaders lose structure, they lose strength. They enter each day reacting instead of directing. Emergencies determine their agenda. Tasks replace purpose. True competence returns through small acts of order: a clear calendar, thoughtful preparation, and honest review. You cannot guide others if you cannot guide your time.

I once visited an organization that described itself as "fast-moving." That phrase appeared in their mission statement and recruitment materials. Yet everything inside moved slowly. Meetings extended without direction. Deadlines slipped. Employees complained quietly about the lack of focus. Leadership blamed the market. The real issue sat in plain sight: they had mistaken momentum for readiness. Real readiness is steady precision, not frantic activity.

Competence declines whenever an organization rewards appearance over improvement. Promotions go to those who are visible rather than impactful. Reports are judged by length instead of clarity. The loudest voice becomes the most influential, even when insight is missing. I have seen excellent ideas dismissed because the presenter was humble, while weaker ideas thrived because they were spoken with confidence. This always weakens an institution from the inside.

Government agencies, universities, and companies show the same pattern. During one consulting assignment, I worked with a ministry where a six-week project had stalled for nearly a year.

Every small action required layers of signatures. Memos moved slowly across hallways. Approvals took weeks. When I asked about the delay, a senior officer said, "We are following procedure." That statement revealed the deeper issue. Procedure without purpose becomes paralysis. Unreadiness at scale often looks like compliance. People avoid risk by avoiding movement. They do not decline responsibility outright. They simply allow time to expire.

This is the crisis of competence. It is not loud failure. It is slow decline. People stop learning. They stop refining their skills. They stop asking questions. The gap between position and preparation widens until institutions are led by titles, not capability.

I once sat through a university board meeting where half an hour was spent debating seating arrangements. We had gathered to discuss national education reform, yet the focus shifted to chairs. That is how unreadiness hides. It directs attention toward the comfortable instead of the necessary.

Through experience, I began to recognize these signals early. They appear in meetings without clear outcomes, in communication filled with delay, in resistance to feedback. A competent leader accepts correction because clarity matters more than pride. An unready leader avoids it because it exposes confusion. Competence fears being unprepared, not being wrong.

A regional executive once shared the challenges facing his division. Revenues were falling. Morale was low. Turnover was high. He blamed external factors for ten minutes. When he finished, I asked a simple question: "When did you last speak directly with the front-line staff?" He paused. Then admitted it had been months. That silence between leader and team is where competence disappears. You cannot change what you refuse to confront.

He took the lesson seriously. He began holding short morning check-ins. He walked through departments and asked direct questions. He listened. The improvement was swift. Productivity rose. Errors declined. Engagement increased. His knowledge had not changed. His presence had. Competence is leadership in motion.

There is also a moral side to competence that many ignore. Technical skill matters, but integrity carries equal weight. The ability to stay calm under pressure, admit mistakes early, choose fairness even when it is unseen — these are the qualities that determine whether competence can be trusted. The greatest damage I have witnessed did not come from lack of intelligence. It came from shortcuts, favoritism, and silence when action was required. Readiness is both operational and ethical.

A moment that shaped my understanding came when advising a new government appointee. He inherited a team burdened by the previous leader's mistakes. Morale was fragile. He told me he wanted to start fresh. I encouraged him to start with humility. Instead of replacing everyone, he listened. He asked questions. He earned trust. Within months, the same team that had resisted him became his strongest supporters. Competence built on respect endures.

During crises, these same principles hold. I once watched a leader publicly blame his team to protect himself. His image improved temporarily. His credibility never recovered. Another leader accepted responsibility for an operational failure that was not entirely his own. He apologized, fixed the issue, and protected his staff. Months later, that team delivered record results. Competence thrives in accountability.

The crisis of competence grows because many systems reward the wrong qualities. Visibility replaces skill. Persuasion replaces preparation. Speed replaces focus. True competence requires time — time to practice judgment, time to learn from failure, time to grow into responsibility. In a world that wants instant results, patience has become rare.

Across every environment I have studied, unreadiness reveals itself through three early signals: overconfidence, disorganization, and silence when accountability is needed. Leaders who cannot self-correct cannot sustain trust. And without trust, competence has no foundation.

Every major leadership failure I have examined follows the same path: unreadiness allowed, competence assumed, accountability delayed, collapse inevitable. That is why I measure readiness not by success, but by recovery. Competent leaders make mistakes, acknowledge them, and learn quickly.

I often remind emerging leaders that competence is revealed in difficult moments. Anyone can appear capable when circumstances are simple. True competence appears when plans fail, pressure rises, and the team looks for direction. I have walked into meetings where everyone looked shaken except one person quietly writing, asking clear questions, and identifying the next step. That person was always the leader, title or not.

Competence begins with habits. It shows up in your preparation, your punctuality, your attention to detail. It shows in how you respond to small setbacks. I once told a group of young professionals that arriving prepared and ready already placed them ahead of half their peers. Small habits become powerful advantages.

Every leader eventually faces a moment when competence is tested. The test does not ask about titles. It asks whether you are prepared to lead when conditions change. Leaders who practice readiness handle those moments with calm. Leaders who ignore readiness fall into panic.

The measure of a leader is not the volume of their voice during calm but the clarity of their thinking during chaos. Success grows from preparation, not luck. The private habits of reading, reflection, order, and humility become the public strength that teams rely on. When those habits fade, even the most capable individuals become unready for the weight they once believed they could carry.

Power Without Readiness

The ballroom filled long before the first spotlight touched the stage. Rows of chairs curved toward the podium, and every seat had been purchased by leaders who expected value. This was not a political event or a government program. It was the annual business conference my consulting company built from the ground up, and it had grown into one of the most influential corporate gatherings in Sub-Saharan Africa. Executives from the country's largest banks sat beside technology leaders, energy CEOs, and the deputy governor of the national monetary authority. Nearly eighty percent of the room consisted of clients who trusted the firm enough to invest in the experience.

What began as a consulting firm had become something more than consultancy work. It formed a bridge between private enterprise, government departments, and regulatory agencies in a way that turned dialogue into real change. The conference became our testing ground for preparation and credibility. I often teach that leadership is not proven through dominance. It is proven through the environments leaders build for others to succeed.

That morning unfolded with deliberate order. The lights softened. The moderator steadied the room. A quiet sense of expectation settled across the hall. For many in the audience, this was another important business event. For me, it represented years of disciplined growth, and a constant reminder of what leadership should protect.

Among the panelists was a man whose name carried significant influence. He was now a respected entrepreneur. I had invited him personally because his insight could elevate the conversation. As he settled into his seat and the applause rose, the moment looked entirely professional. Yet for me, it opened a doorway into a different season of my life.

Years earlier, before the consulting firm, before the standing and credibility, I had faced this same man in a much smaller hall. The setting was a faith-based community where I volunteered. A kind welfare officer had noticed that my shoes were worn. Without prompting, he handed me a donated pair. I thanked him, never imagining that a simple act of generosity would reveal a lesson about power.

A week later, during a large gathering attended by hundreds, the head of the organization — the same man now seated on my stage — called me forward. I assumed it was for a routine task. Instead, he asked publicly where I got the shoes. When I explained, he summoned the welfare officer and ordered that the shoes be taken from me. He instructed him to replace them with worn flip-flops.

The room grew tense. I had done nothing wrong. The shoes had been offered freely. Yet I stood there in silence as the pair was removed and replaced. In that moment, I learned a truth that shaped my leadership for years to come. Power without readiness injures the people who trust it. It does not inspire. It intimidates. It masks insecurity behind authority.

I walked home that night when the flip-flops broke on the road. Each step pushed the lesson deeper into my thinking. Leadership is not the right to command. It is the responsibility to protect. I made a quiet promise that anyone who crossed my path would leave my presence with dignity intact.

I was never impoverished in the material sense. My family lived comfortably. My personal hardship during that period was a choice. I wanted to build from zero. I wanted to understand effort without inherited advantage. That discipline gave me perspective long before I held responsibility.

Every difficult experience offers two options. Resentment drains progress. Refinement builds wisdom. I chose refinement. That moment of humiliation, as unfair as it felt, became a masterclass in leadership long before I entered a boardroom.

Years later, as that same man stepped onto my conference stage, I felt no anger. Only clarity. The experience that once wounded me had become the reason I led with a different spirit. I watched him speak with confidence while the audience listened closely. I sat in the front row, no longer the young man with broken flip-flops, but the founder who built the platform that now hosted him. Success had changed the environment. Character had changed the meaning.

When the session ended, I thanked him publicly and acknowledged his contribution like every other panelist. That was my victory. Not over him. Over the resentment that could have shaped me. Power had returned to my hands, and I chose grace instead of pride.

That moment strengthened my understanding of readiness. Leadership is not tested when supervision is present. It is tested when no one can intervene. The behaviors seen in private shape the outcomes seen in public.

The conference itself reflected that principle. Attendees did not attend for knowledge alone. They invested in credibility and trust. We created an environment where every participant felt respected, regardless of their title. Influence was shared with discipline, not ego. Decisions were guided by clarity, not showmanship.

As the firm expanded, I built that principle into our culture. We trained clients on systems and operational excellence, while also teaching them the behaviors that sustain institutions. I emphasized that unreadiness is not simply a lack of skill. It is a lack of conscience. The welfare officer who gave me those shoes had readiness. He saw a need and responded. The leader who took them away lacked readiness. He saw difference and used it to diminish.

That insight reshaped our programs. We developed what I called dignity protocols — practical habits that ensured people were treated with respect at every level. In corporations, public offices, and schools, the rule remained constant. Authority cannot maintain influence if it damages dignity.

Power without readiness becomes empty noise. Readiness without conscience becomes routine ceremony. True leadership requires both competence and character.

That day on the conference stage, I saw both sides clearly. One leader's unreadiness had injured. Another leader's growth had forgiven. The distance between those choices was not circumstance. It was development.

As I looked across the audience — executives, policymakers, investors — I realized that their greatest need was not more data. It was a model of disciplined leadership. They needed to see that greatness is measured not by applause but by how power is held when no one can challenge it.

From that point onward, I designed every leadership program, client engagement, and partnership around a single principle. Maturity protects dignity before it seeks influence. That perspective strengthened relationships, built loyalty, and shaped a culture where people performed with commitment instead of compliance.

Over time, another truth emerged. Readiness is not a one-time accomplishment. It is a daily responsibility. Leaders lose it the moment ego replaces empathy. When that happens, institutions weaken as quickly as individuals do.

That moment on the conference stage became more than memory. It became method. It taught me that unreadiness does not stay contained in people. It spreads through the systems they build. When systems fail to prepare, even well-intentioned people eventually fall short.

***

Every generation believes it is ready until history asks the questions it never practiced. Moments that seem manageable from a distance often reveal the truth about preparation. Yet a deeper issue shapes many of the challenges we see today. It is the fading of what I call leadership memory, the carried wisdom that once helped each new group of leaders avoid the mistakes of the ones before them. Institutions that were built on steady mentorship, apprenticeship-style learning, and gradual transitions now push people into authority without proximity to seasoned guidance. Turnover rises, schedules tighten, and the support structure that once helped developing leaders mature disappears. We expect insight from the unmentored and call it a personal failure when it does not appear, instead of recognizing that the system failed to equip them.

Leadership memory is not a clerical function. It is the practical knowledge, habits, and judgment passed from experienced leaders to emerging ones — the kind of understanding that cannot be found in manuals or policies. When it disappears, institutions repeat errors that could have been prevented. This goes far beyond staffing concerns. It touches the nation's resilience. The leaders who guide education, health, finance, public safety, and innovation form the human infrastructure of the country. When preparation is absent, the systems they manage weaken. When weakness becomes familiar, expectations fall. People begin to expect very little from those elected, appointed, or hired. That quiet resignation is far more dangerous than visible dysfunction because it shapes culture.

The signs of unreadiness are already visible. Decisions stall because no one wants to risk being wrong. Policies are recycled because no one knows how to create new ones. Meetings end with more questions than direction. Many rising leaders feel the strain but struggle to name it. They describe the experience instead: overwhelmed, undertrained, unsupported, and alone.

Repairing this requires more than updated workshops or revised performance reviews. It demands a new understanding of readiness itself. Leadership must be seen as a discipline that requires practice, not as a reward granted at the end of a career.

Mentorship must return as a normal expectation. Leadership memory must be restored so wisdom carries forward rather than vanishing with each transition. People preparing for complex roles need scenario practice, systems fluency, and honest engagement with the responsibilities they will hold. Readiness must be built long before promotion, not assumed the moment authority is given.

The issue facing the country is not only declining trust in institutions. It is the fading belief that anyone is genuinely prepared. When the public no longer trusts that capable leadership exists, the vacuum fills quickly. It is filled by entertainers, by movements driven more by frustration than understanding, and by noise that crowds out thoughtful guidance.

Silence about readiness creates space for substitutes. And substitutes, once elevated, rarely step aside without disruption. Rebuilding readiness will take time, yet it begins with acknowledging the issue without blame or defensiveness. The challenge is larger than a few underperforming leaders. It reflects a national model that no longer equips people for the complexity they inherit. I have watched this gap appear in boardrooms, public departments, and national initiatives, and the solutions become clear whenever institutions invest in the quiet disciplines that sustain leadership.

Readiness is the unseen backbone behind every lasting achievement. When it weakens, collapse becomes a question of time. Progress in business, government, and service depends on leaders who are prepared before they are elevated. The question is no longer whether preparation is necessary. The question is when it will begin. The opportunity sits before us now, and the window will not remain open forever.

TWO

THE MISSING LINK AT THE SUMMIT

The quiet decay that began underneath the surface eventually reached the highest floor of leadership. In the middle of an organization, delays look like confusion. At the summit, delay becomes drift. Approvals that should be held for a week dissolve before Friday afternoon. Deputies who could lead choose to remain one level down because the office above them offers attention without stability. From a distance, the summit looks strong. Up close, it can feel like a narrow plank suspended over open water.

In every high-stakes system, continuity is treated as non-negotiable. When the President of the United States undergoes a routine medical procedure that requires sedation, authority transfers immediately. During major national events, a designated successor waits safely at an undisclosed location. These measures are not symbolic. They are structural safeguards. The Situation Room exists so decisions are anticipated rather than improvised. Continuity is engineered long before the moment that requires it.

Many institutions do not follow this standard. They depend on assumption. Tenure is mistaken for judgment. Academic credentials substitute for discernment. A confident speaker is confused with a steady decision maker. Titles offer visibility but not always skill. The decision that is resolved on Monday returns for debate on Friday because a senior leader returns from travel and wants a different price, a different approach, or a different explanation. When this becomes routine, the center of the institution weakens. People begin to wait for reversals. Momentum stalls.

I witnessed this repeatedly through my consulting firm. Our reputation grew because we advised the top players in banking and insurance. These clients were national anchors, institutions that measured influence by the markets they shaped. They came to us because we produced measurable improvement in performance and structure. They did not seek motivation. They sought results that could be seen in their financial records. I never told them what they preferred to hear. I told them what they needed to advance, and that is why they remained loyal.

One engagement involved the insurance subsidiary of a top-three African bank, a financial group with more than a century of history. The subsidiary's CEO and his management team approved a major product-strategy project after my presentation. Every detail was clear. The scope, the timeline, and the value were agreed. The agreement was sealed. The partnership was designed to modernize their portfolio and strengthen their competitiveness in a fast-changing market.

Execution rested with the parent group at the bank's headquarters. That was where the fault line appeared. A senior executive who was not involved with the division returned from leave and instructed her team to reopen negotiations. The change had nothing to do with quality or alignment. She simply wanted the same value at a reduced price because she had not been present at the earlier decision. The reversal revealed the danger of symbolic authority. It was not a financial issue. It was a matter of principle. Once value is agreed and commitments are in place, reversing the terms is not prudent. It is erosion.

I declined. People who understand value seldom ask for discounts. People who do not understand value cannot recognize what they are losing. Some describe my firm as expensive. I describe it as measurable. Productivity, value, and results have numbers attached to them. My clients see those numbers. That is why they return.

When the summit cannot protect its own commitments, the organization cannot protect its standards. Every reversal signals that authority is uncertain and consistency is optional. No institution remains strong under those conditions.

Years later, the same subsidiary attended one of our leadership and market-intelligence programs. It was a national gathering with more than one hundred and fifty senior executives from banks and insurers across Africa. Participants flew in from cities across the continent. Each one paid premium fee because they came for insight that could be applied immediately.

More than sixty percent of my clients request exclusivity. They want private sessions for their teams, their own branding in the room, and insights that remain internal. In highly competitive markets, exclusivity becomes a strategic asset. It also requires the investment that supports it.

The subsidiary's CEO approached me again. He asked for an exclusive session for his team, separate from the main program, but he did not want to pay the fee that exclusivity required. I declined. Relationships create flexibility. They never erase fairness. Value has to remain consistent, or credibility disappears.

That decision protected more than pricing. It protected trust. Integrity in business is not measured through how flexible you appear. It is measured through fairness and consistency. The following year, the bank merged the subsidiary into a larger competitor. The same CEO who pursued exclusivity without investment retired soon after. Prestige without structure rarely holds when pressure arrives.

Those experiences shaped my understanding of continuity at the summit. Authority must not only command. It must sustain. When leaders at the top cannot protect their own standards, continuity fractures quietly. What appears stable from the outside begins to weaken within.

Organizations that endure approach continuity the way the United States approaches national security. They build systems that make readiness routine. They practice judgment, not ceremony. They document the reasoning behind important decisions, so the next leader inherits understanding, not only position. They pass on judgment, not just authority.

This became the foundation of what I taught leaders who sought depth rather than visibility. Continuity is not a slogan. It is a design principle. It must live inside the practices of an institution. You cannot prepare for crisis in the middle of crisis. Preparation must come before pressure. The designated successor is identified before the emergency, not after it. The Situation Room gathers before the problem, not during it.

Institutions that last think the same way. They do not assume stability. They build it. They protect the chain of decisions so a single reversal cannot paralyze motion. They ensure that authority leads to action, not performance. They rehearse response long before the headline appears.

Continuity is never accidental. It belongs to leaders who return stronger after strain. It shows up in the nurse who steadies her hands during another difficult night in the ICU, the athlete who lifts again after a failed attempt, the skydiver who steps back into the aircraft after a hard landing. Leadership readiness is proven under pressure. Credentials prepare. Presentation impresses. Judgment under constraint sustains. Leaders who carry that level of resilience create organizations that endure. They become the anchors every summit requires.

When institutions understand this truth, they stop waiting for pressure to reveal readiness. They begin building it.

The Poverty Plate

Long before I advised executives or stood on stages before national audiences, I learned my first real lesson in unreadiness. It came not in a boardroom, but at a buffet.

I was a teenager when I was invited to a faith leadership gathering at one of the finest hotels in the city. The environment was new to me. My family lived well, but I had never stepped into a setting that combined elegance with formality. I was modest in every way. I spoke little, observed more, and carried myself quietly. The invitation felt like a door into a world I had only seen from afar.

I arrived that morning wearing an oversized brown jacket that had passed through several hands before it reached me. The shoulders sat wide, the seams were worn, yet it was clean and pressed. As I walked through the marble lobby, chandeliers reflected off polished floors and guests moved with a confidence I did not yet understand. I reminded myself that belonging depended more on attitude than appearance.

After the morning session, lunch was announced. The buffet stretched across the hall like a celebration. Dishes I had never tasted stood beside desserts I had only seen in photographs. I joined the line with my plate in hand, and in my excitement, I took everything. Rice, chicken, fish, salad, fruit, pastries. I stacked my plate until it could hold no more.

When I sat among the dignitaries, I noticed that my plate looked frantic while theirs looked measured. They ate calmly and spoke quietly. I ate quickly, hoping no one would notice the difference. Heat gathered under my jacket. My breathing grew tight. In that moment, I understood what unreadiness feels like: wanting to belong, yet not knowing how to carry yourself when the opportunity finally arrives.

My embarrassment was not about clothing or background. It came from realizing that I had been invited to a table I was not prepared to handle. The lesson stayed with me. Opportunity without preparation reveals more than it rewards.

In time, I saw how organizations repeat the same mistake. They load their plates with more than they can sustain. They pursue every partnership, accept every project, and chase every possibility because they believe the chance may never come again. They confuse activity with achievement. Excellence has never been measured by how much you collect. It is measured by how wisely you choose.

Hunger without discipline turns potential into waste. Passion without preparation turns access into exposure.

The buffet was never about food. It was about formation. Every platform amplifies both strength and weakness. People rise to the level of their preparation, not the level of their desire. Invitations reveal what has been practiced in private.

I returned home that day and made a quiet promise. I would never again arrive at a table unprepared. If life opened a door, I would walk through it with discipline and composure. That single promise shaped how I learned, worked, and built habits. Before accepting responsibility, I asked myself whether I had earned the right to carry it. Before stepping into opportunity, I asked whether my habits matched the level of the room.

Readiness begins in honest self-assessment, not in applause.

Over the years, I met leaders who reminded me of that moment at the buffet. They were talented and sincere, yet had never been taught the etiquette of opportunity. They were promoted early, praised quickly, and when real responsibility arrived, they froze. They filled their calendars with commitments they could not keep and initiatives they could not complete. Their hunger was genuine. Their systems were weak.

What I learned that day was simple. Hunger is not the enemy. It simply needs maturity. Mature hunger becomes purpose. Immature hunger becomes panic.

Leadership is not in how much you acquire. It is in how steady you remain when abundance appears.

Readiness, I discovered, is not a talent. It is a temperament. It is the calm that comes from preparation long before recognition arrives.

When I eventually began leading major initiatives and hosting high-level conferences, that early lesson became my anchor. I understood the weight of walking into a room that demanded more than enthusiasm. Visibility without preparation is exposure, not success.

I saw the same unreadiness at the highest levels of institutions. Boards chased every opportunity. Departments drowned in projects. Leaders collected titles without building systems. Each one mirrored that buffet table. The problem was not ambition. It was the absence of appetite management.

Preparation is the invisible work that turns visible moments into competence.

That is the paradox of leadership. The quiet labor that no one celebrates determines who stands steady when the moment arrives.

As I grew, I recognized that unreadiness appears in many forms. Some leaders overcommit. Others become perfectionists. Many operate from fear of scarcity, convinced that if they do not take everything now, they may never get another chance. That mindset does not come from lack of money. It comes from insecurity. It whispers the same message: take it all, because the table may not return.

Stewardship corrects that message. It teaches that what belongs to you will meet you at the right time if you are faithful. It turns emotion into discipline and opportunity into responsibility.

Leaders who operate from stewardship protect value before expanding it. They build systems rather than chase symbols. They prepare quietly so they can lead calmly.

That is the maturity that separates leaders who endure from those who only appear successful.

Prepared leaders do not rush to fill their plate. They pause. They observe. They honor the moment. They understand that abundance is not the time to indulge. It is the time to demonstrate restraint.

In every field I later served, the most prepared leaders were the most composed. They did not equate access with arrival. They understood that each opportunity, each board seat, each new project was its own buffet that tested the discipline of readiness.

Preparation before promotion. Readiness before recognition.

That is the sequence that never fails.

As institutions adopt that mindset, trust rises. Decisions sharpen. Performance becomes predictable. Individuals who adopt it stop chasing validation. They begin cultivating mastery.

That afternoon at the buffet marked a turning point. I realized that every leader must choose how they will behave at the table of opportunity. Some grab everything. Others choose wisely. Composure becomes the real currency.

Years later, when I worked with CEOs, regulators, and public leaders, I often thought back to that moment. The setting had changed. The principle had not. Readiness still separated those who lasted from those who faded.

The lesson has never expired.

That day taught me the first half of the principle: preparation before promotion. The years that followed revealed the second: steadiness under strain.

The next lesson arrived miles above the ground, inside a quiet cabin where engines faltered and patience thinned. It was a moment that showed me calm is rarer than talent and that judgment under pressure is the true test of a leader.

Locked on the Tarmac

The flight from Amsterdam to the United States was scheduled for late evening. I had been traveling for days through London and other cities, meeting leaders, reviewing strategy, and speaking late into the night. My body was tired, yet my mind stayed alert. When I settled into my seat, I told myself this flight would be my only quiet hour. It did not turn out that way.

Minutes after the door closed, the captain made an announcement. There was an issue with one of the engines. He believed it would be resolved shortly. The crew moved with practiced confidence, yet the air in the cabin began to shift. The temperature climbed. Air circulation stopped. The smell of fuel lingered. Children started to cry. Grown men raised their voices. You could feel tension growing with every passing minute.

The captain returned with another update. The test had failed. A second test also failed. A third followed the same path. Each time, his voice remained steady. He did not promise what he could not guarantee. He did not fill the silence with unnecessary comfort. He reported what he knew, explained what would be attempted next, and let truth fill the gap where panic could have taken hold.

That silence became a lesson I never forgot. Leadership is not proven when everything works. It is revealed when everything stalls. The captain showed that calm carries more influence than authority. His discipline filled the space more than the rising heat.

Three hours passed before the final test succeeded. The same passengers who had shouted earlier now sat quietly, exhausted but safe. When the aircraft finally lifted off, no one applauded. People simply absorbed the truth that calm had carried us.

That night became one of my strongest metaphors for leadership under strain. The cockpit, unseen by most, held the weight of every decision. The captain's steadiness reminded me that leadership is not about privilege. It is about responsibility.

Leaders across every industry face their own version of a grounded aircraft. The failing engine might be a stalled launch, an unexpected crisis, a breach of trust, or a public challenge that many underestimated. The crew might be employees demanding answers or board members growing anxious. The pressure to promise what cannot be guaranteed is enormous. That is when genuine leadership stands apart.

Every institution needs someone who can stay composed when the temperature rises. Anyone can appear decisive when conditions are ideal. The real test is whether a leader can protect judgment when frustration grows and uncertainty hangs over the room.

The captain had not discovered calm in that moment. He had built it long before that night. Years of training had shaped a voice that remained steady even while systems failed. That is the same principle organizations forget. In times of crisis, teams need communication that is honest, timely, and clear. They do not need dramatic speeches. They need accuracy.

I later translated that insight into consulting practice. During leadership workshops, I often asked executives to simulate the first hour of a crisis. What would be their first call? What would be their first sentence to the staff? What would they communicate to the public if all eyes were on them? The early rounds were often hesitant. Voices wavered. Phrases circled without direction. Yet after a few repetitions, clarity replaced confusion. Everyone discovered that calm can be trained.

Organizations that cultivate this discipline recover faster. They lose less trust because their communication remains human. People can forgive delay when integrity is visible. Structured repetition under stress becomes a sign of reliability, not rigidity.

That flight taught me that clarity eases fear more than comfort. The captain never offered promises he could not uphold. He gave truth in steady steps. That is leadership in its most honest form, when accuracy becomes assurance.

The same reality holds inside organizations. Executives often believe they must speak constantly to show control. In truth, confidence grows when leaders speak only when their information is verified. A team's belief in its leader is shaped not in moments of success, but in the moments when the leader's voice stays calm while uncertainty grows.

Aviation carries another lesson. Aircrews train to protect process from emotion. They use checklists because fatigue can alter memory. Strong organizations follow the same pattern. They create systems that guard judgment during emotional moments. They train deputies to communicate with authority so steadiness never depends on one person.

The cockpit also teaches something subtle. Each failed test could have embarrassed the captain. Instead, he treated each result as information. He did not see failure. He saw data. That mindset separates mature organizations from reactive ones. Mature institutions treat setbacks as direction. Immature institutions treat them as threats to image.

That understanding helped me later when I guided leadership teams to record the reasoning behind their toughest decisions. The purpose was not to assign blame. It was to preserve institutional judgment. Those records became living references for the next generation, turning setbacks into instruction. The most capable organizations do this naturally. They know that memory is not a file. It is active practice.

The captain also revealed another truth. Fatigue tests integrity. When people are tired, they trade principles for relief. They speak too quickly. They decide too fast. They lose patience. That is why recovery is a strategic discipline. Fatigue is not passive. It reshapes judgment. The captain's composure rested on the resilience he built long before that night.

When we finally took off, the lesson was complete. Calm leadership is a reflex trained over time. Knowledge recites the checklist. Wisdom keeps its voice steady while reading it.

I have seen this truth in hospitals, boardrooms, and public agencies. The nurse who steadies her hands through a long night carries the same discipline as the athlete who makes another attempt after a failed lift. The skydiver who returns to the plane after a hard landing demonstrates the same resolve as the pilot who refuses to rush through protocol. Readiness is revealed under pressure.

Organizations that endure are built by leaders who learn to stay composed in their cockpit moments. They hold their tone when others lose theirs. They preserve trust when shortcuts tempt. They anchor institutions through their steadiness.

often tell executives that reputation is built in quiet moments. The meeting no one will remember—the one where you stayed measured while others drifted—is often the moment your credibility was established. The best leaders protect their brand through composure, not slogans.

Every leader eventually faces a grounded aircraft. A stalled project, a divided team, a financial delay, or a public challenge. That is where readiness separates the steady from the fragile.

When we landed, I understood the difference between information and wisdom. Information explains the process. Wisdom keeps the voice steady while the process is tested.

The next turbulence I faced was in the business world, where a venture carried potential yet lacked the structure to support it. The lesson unfolded quietly, showing me that enthusiasm without design collapses, no matter the talent or vision behind it.

The Venture That Would Not Stand

I had every visible advantage. Years on the microphone had taught me how to frame ideas with precision. Five days a week I spoke live across six radio stations. Brands paid for those minutes because trust converts. When I endorsed a product, phone lines moved and counters clicked. In many ways I was a bridge between the market and the people who served it. That credibility made e-commerce feel like a natural extension. If I could help companies win attention, I could build a platform that turned attention into orders and orders into loyalty.

I moved quickly. I secured premium suppliers in Turkey and began exploratory conversations in China. Logistics ran through UPS. Our content was sharp, our positioning clear, our inventory curated. We were not trying to be everything to everyone. We would stand for quality customers did not have to second-guess. The marketing engine was already in motion. I did not need to buy a spotlight. I had earned one over years of disciplined broadcasts.

For a time the signals were all green. Traffic grew. The brand felt strong in the mouth when people said it. Customers wrote with gratitude. Partners wanted placement. We built campaigns that carried the voice of the shows into a storefront that looked the part. To anyone watching, the path was predictable: visibility would become velocity, velocity would become dominance, dominance would become profit.

Then reality introduced itself without ceremony. Competitors flooded the market with poor-quality goods priced below cost. Investor money fueled loss-leading tactics that had no regard for sustainability. They were not selling products; they were buying time and attention by burning capital. One competitor eventually sold for a single dollar because there was nothing left to sell but a logo and a mailing list. The signal we had trusted—rising demand—was distorted by a noise we had underestimated: artificial pricing that trained customers to believe the floor was the ceiling.

I held to a premium product at a moderate price because trust had built my career. I would not break that trust now. But the unit economics pushed back. Each week brought the same negotiation with reality. Marketing could make a promise. Operations had to keep it. Operations kept it, but at a cost the market refused to meet. After nearly three years, I made the decision to shut the venture down.

People asked whether it was a failure. I called it tuition. I had paid in money, time, and pride to learn a lesson I now teach often. Visibility is not viability. A strong voice without a strong design turns momentum into turbulence. You cannot scale presentation. You can only scale process.

The hardest part was not closing the doors. The hardest part was telling the team. They believed in the mission because I had sold it with conviction. That day required a different kind of honesty.

I told them the model was sincere in intention and weak in structure. We could continue and risk losing trust, or we could stop and keep it. I chose to keep it, because trust is the one asset you can never repurchase once it is spent carelessly.

That decision changed the way I build anything that carries my name. Before I commit to scale, I now insist on seeing the spine. I want to see the consistent pace that will carry weight when enthusiasm cools. I want to see the rules that will hold when the room asks for shortcuts. I want to see the numbers that refuse to flatter me. If a plan cannot survive these tests, it is not a plan. It is a wish.

Leaders often confuse demand with durability. Demand is a photograph. Durability is a film. Demand tells you today's story. Durability tells you how the story ends. My venture had photographs anyone would frame. It did not have the film a disciplined builder would trust. I believed what the market said to my face and ignored what it whispered behind my back. The face said yes. The whisper asked how.

That insight reshaped how I advise founders and public officials standing at the edge of new ideas. I ask them to show me the choreography, not the poster. Posters sell nights. Choreography sustains seasons. What happens when a supplier misses two cycles in a row. Who has the authority to stop a promotion when economics no longer justify it. Which prices protect the brand's voice in a customer's mind. Who speaks first when a campaign misfires and customers are angry for reasons that are not entirely fair. If the answers are short and confident, you are ready. If the answers depend on the calendar, the next meeting, or the return of someone who travels often, you have not designed for continuity. You have designed for hope.

My radio years had trained a different muscle that I had not fully transplanted into the venture. Live airtime tolerates nothing sloppy. You prepare, perform, and honor the clock. The discipline that made those segments strong should have been the discipline that shaped our operating pattern. Fifteen minutes, five times a week, built a habit of arriving ready. I needed the same consistency in inventory planning, cash control, and service recovery. Not inspiration on Monday and improvisation on Friday, but a consistent pace that made excellence normal and panic rare.

So I wrote a rule I still use today. Every dream earns its routine or it becomes a regret. Routine is not the enemy of creativity. Routine is the scaffold that lets creativity climb.

There were bright spots I would not trade. We learned how to write clearer copy because customers teach you how they decide. We learned which promises matter and which ones only sound good in meetings. We learned that a small apology delivered quickly protects more loyalty than an elaborate gesture delivered late. We learned that the right words can spark interest, but only the right systems can build a reputation.

What should a leader carry from this into a company that looks healthy on paper. Carry the refusal to be fooled by attention. Carry the habit of asking for the backbone before approving the billboard. Carry the discipline of measuring what a customer repeats to a friend after the first-purchase glow fades. Carry the courage to close what is attractive but unstable so you can build what is strong.

There is a moment in every endeavor when the arithmetic asks for an answer the heart does not want to give. That is when leadership either protects the future or mortgages it. Protecting the future sometimes means pausing the present. It means telling your people what they already sense and proving with your choices that your standards are not for sale, not even to your own optimism.

After I closed the venture, I sat in a quiet office and wrote two pages I still keep. The first listed the signals I trusted that did not deserve trust. The second listed the questions I did not ask because the early success was flattering. Those pages became a private curriculum. They turned scars into a system. The system now lives as a checklist in my mind before I invest energy in anything new. If the checklist says we are not ready, I do not argue with it. I adjust the plan or walk away.

What changed in me was not ambition. Ambition stayed. What changed was the shape of my ambition. I stopped reaching for the next stage until the stage beneath me could carry twice my weight. I stopped believing that speed is the same as progress. I stopped speaking in superlatives when the team needed sequences. I started insisting that every proud sentence be matched with a quiet sentence that began with how.

A leader's job is not to keep hope alive at any cost. A leader's job is to keep hope honest. When hope is honest, even hard news strengthens the room, because people can trust the ground beneath their feet. They may not like the path, but they will walk it with you.

In the years after the closure, I noticed something interesting. Customers still wrote to thank us. They were not thanking us for shoes or clothes. They were thanking us for honesty. They were grateful that we treated them as people who deserved truth, not targets who deserved spin. That is the signature I want my name to carry in any market: clear, steady, trustworthy. It does not always shout. It always lasts.

The lesson is simple to say and costly to keep. Do not let visibility seduce you into skipping design. Do not let a strong start convince you that gravity has changed. Gravity respects no one. It pulls on everyone the same. The only way to rise and stay up is to build a structure that respects the pull and still climbs.

There is a quiet sentence I repeat when a new opportunity looks beautiful and the room is excited. Beauty does not guarantee balance. I repeat it again when the early numbers look kind and the press wants a quote. Kind numbers do not guarantee keepable numbers. I repeat it a third time when a respected friend says I am being too strict. Strict standards are not enemies of growth. They are its guardians.

The e-commerce venture did not break my stride. It taught me where strong strides come from. They come from ankles supported by routine. They come from legs that know when to bend and when to hold. They come from a frame that remembers alignment when terrain changes. In leadership the anatomy is the same. Progress comes from the small choices you make each week that no one applauds but everyone feels.

The venture taught me something else. Readiness is not words. It is behavior under weight.

When organizations absorb that truth, everything improves. Succession becomes a transfer of judgment, not just of keys. Strategy becomes decisions supported by the reasoning behind them, so the next person can think in the same lanes when conditions change. Culture becomes a consistent pace people can count on, not a speech people forget.

The venture that would not stand gave me a gift I did not expect. It gave me a scar that points the way. Whenever I am tempted to scale a feeling, I look at that scar. It reminds me to scale a system instead. Feelings tire. Good systems grow stronger with use.

I closed the books and walked into the next season with steadier footing. Calm in crisis. Design before scale. Consistent pace every week. Protect the name. If we keep those four, the rest arrives in time.

Learning Beside Real Decisions

The lessons from the plate at the hotel, the hot cabin on the tarmac, and the venture that could not stand did more than shape how I think. They changed how I develop people.

I came to see that judgment does not grow in isolation. It grows beside real decisions. People do not learn steadiness from memos. They learn it from watching someone hold a line when money is at stake, when reputation is involved, and when the easy answer would win applause.

When I began to build teams, I made a simple choice. I opened the door.

Younger colleagues sat in on client sessions, internal reviews, and negotiations where the outcome could move a budget or reshape a plan. Often they did not say a word. Their assignment was to watch and listen. They were watching more than the words. They watched how I paused before agreeing to a request. They watched how I handled a demand that sounded impressive but did not make sense. They watched how I declined work that would burn time without building value.

After those meetings, we sat down for a short debrief. I usually asked one question.

"What did you notice when the conversation became uncomfortable."

Their answers showed me what they were really learning. They saw that a leader can say no without disrespect. They saw that staying calm is not weakness. They saw that protecting a standard sometimes means walking away from easy income. Those moments taught more than any slide deck.

Every serious field uses some version of this pattern. A junior lawyer sits at counsel table and listens to a senior attorney argue a motion. A resident shadows an experienced physician during a long night and watches how decisions are made when everyone is tired. A young officer rides with a commander and sees how they speak to people in the middle of conflict. Skill moves from theory to instinct through proximity.

Leadership is no different. Rising leaders need to see the real thing. They need to see a budget meeting where someone simply says, "We are not going to hit this number safely unless we remove these promises." They need to see a hiring decision where competence is strong but character is not trusted, and the answer is no. They need to see a leader admit, "I chose wrong there," and then fix it without drama.

That is what I call leadership memory. It is not a slogan or a diagram. It is the living record of how wise people handled hard choices. When that record is visible, new leaders inherit more than a job description. They inherit a way of thinking.

Where this is missing, people arrive at senior roles with very little lived guidance. They know what the policy says, yet they have never watched it stand up under strain. That is how titles expand while judgment shrinks.

The remedy begins with access. Senior leaders have to treat proximity as part of their duty, not as a favor. Pull up an extra chair. Invite a younger leader to sit through the tough meeting, not only the celebration. Answer questions afterward. Explain why you held a line or changed your mind. Over time, this one habit turns isolated insight into shared wisdom.

Continuity does not start with a binder. It starts with someone who is willing to let others see how real decisions are made.

Sponsorship That Costs Something

Watching is not enough. At some point, a leader must do more than explain decisions. A leader must trust someone else to make one.

The turning point in a person's growth often arrives in a single sentence.
"This one is yours. I will stand behind you."

There is a clear difference between mentoring and sponsorship. Mentoring is advice. It can happen over coffee, on a video call, or in passing conversation. It is helpful and often sincere. Sponsorship is different. Sponsorship is when a senior leader attaches their name to someone's actual work, in a setting where the results will be seen and measured.

Mentoring says, "Here is what I would do."
Sponsorship says, "You will do it, and my reputation will stand beside you."

I remember the first time I made that decision with a young manager in one of my ventures. She had been in the room for many briefings. She had taken careful notes and offered good insight afterward. One day a key session was scheduled. Instead of leading it myself, I told her, "You will handle this briefing. I am here, but I will not step in unless you lose control of the room."

We prepared fully. We walked through tough questions in advance. We agreed on what she would protect and what she could adjust. When the meeting started, I sat slightly back and watched. She opened clearly, answered challenges without defensiveness, and admitted one gap without trying to blame anyone. The client left with confidence. She left with something even more important. She now knew she could hold a room that mattered.

Afterward, I told her, "Today was not about the file. Today was about your name."

This is the heart of sponsorship. It is not a kind word in the hallway. It is not a coffee conversation about ambition. It is the decision to put real work, real risk, and real visibility in someone's hands while your own credibility is tied to the outcome.

In healthy organizations, sponsorship is not a secret practice. It is a visible habit. Senior leaders can name the people they are currently backing in real assignments. These assignments are not errands. They are projects that carry consequences. A sponsored leader might run an important client presentation, lead a cross functional initiative, or stand in front of the board to explain a plan. The senior leader remains available yet does not take over. The younger leader carries the moment.

This changes the way people grow. They work differently when they know someone has placed trust on the line for them. They prepare more deeply. They notice details they once ignored. They feel the weight of the decision and learn to stand up under it.

Sponsorship also reveals a culture's honesty. If senior people cannot point to anyone whose development is tied to them, then continuity is already weak. The summit may look busy, yet it is not building a future. When the only plan for senior vacancies is to hire from outside, the institution is only renting continuity. It is not producing it.

There is another trap to avoid. Some leaders confuse sponsorship with favoritism. Favoritism gives chances without standards. Sponsorship gives chances with clear expectations. The difference rests in transparency and fairness. When sponsorship is healthy, criteria are clear. People know that trust is earned through integrity, consistent effort, and steady results, not through flattery or social closeness.

One practical tool I often recommend is simple. Ask each executive to keep a short list with two names. Those two names represent people they are actively sponsoring in visible work this year. With each name, write the assignment, the risk, and the support being provided. Review that list as seriously as you review financial targets. This does more than grow individuals. It sends a message throughout the organization. Growth is not random. Growth is a shared responsibility.

True sponsorship demands something from both sides. The sponsor accepts that their own reputation is now tied to the protégé's performance. The protégé accepts that excuses will not carry weight. The assignment is not a simulation. The result matters. That shared awareness is where maturity forms fastest.

I have seen sponsored leaders rise far beyond their first supporters. Some now lead teams and institutions larger than anything I once managed. I have also seen sponsored leaders stumble in public. Both outcomes taught valuable lessons. Success showed that standards travel well. Failure showed where development still needed work and what systems were missing. In both cases, the organization learned more than it would have learned through another round of training slides.

Sponsorship is the missing link in many high-level environments. There is plenty of talk, plenty of coaching language, and plenty of informal mentoring. There is not enough visible transfer of real authority with real stakes.

Where sponsorship becomes normal, continuity stops being a slogan. It becomes a chain of tested people who know how it feels to carry weight before the crisis, not during it.

Closing the Gap at the Summit

Looking back across the stories in this section, the pattern is clear.

A teenager stood at a buffet table and discovered that opportunity without preparation exposes more than it elevates.

A plane sat on the tarmac while a captain stayed calm through repeated tests and taught an entire cabin what leadership sounds like when nothing moves.

An e commerce venture with strong attention and weak design closed with dignity and turned into a private curriculum that guides decisions to this day.

Younger leaders stepped into rooms where real tradeoffs were made and saw how standards are defended.

Sponsored leaders carried work that could succeed or fail in public, while a senior name quietly stood behind them.

Each scene points to the same truth. Readiness is not theory. It is behavior underweight, and it must exist at the top if a nation wants a deep bench of capable leaders.

This matters far beyond any single company. The people who lead hospitals, schools, banks, agencies, and fast-growing firms form a large part of a country's working strength. When they are well prepared, the systems under them can improve. When they are unprepared, those systems become brittle. Over time, citizens begin to lower their expectations. They stop believing that anyone is truly ready. That quiet loss of confidence is one of the most dangerous forms of decline.

The gap is not only a skills gap. It is a continuity gap. Many professionals work hard at the base and the middle. They study. They grind. They carry more than their job title suggests. When promotion finally arrives, they discover that no one has prepared them to stand at the summit. They have talent. They have drive. They have not been given structured proximity and real sponsorship.

Closing that gap requires more than new programs. It requires a different mindset at the top.

Senior leaders must see themselves not only as decision makers, but as stewards of judgment. They must invite others into the room when the choices are hard. They must place real assignments in new hands while staying close enough to guide.

They must treat continuity as part of their daily work, not as a paragraph in a report.

On the personal side, each leader must decide what kind of foundation they want to stand on. Talent and energy are important. They are not enough. The leaders who endure at the summit share two habits.

They prepare for opportunities that have not yet appeared.

They treat trust as a form of capital that must never be spent carelessly.

Effort alone does not close America's talent gap. Effort combined with readiness and trust does.

In my own journey, every door that stayed open shared the same pattern. Hard work prepared the ground. Trust decided how far the opportunity would travel. Clients, partners, and audiences did not stay because of charm. They stayed because, over time, they could predict what my decisions would protect.

That is the path that links continuity at the summit with the life of a single leader. Institutions become stronger when individuals live that way. Individuals advance further when institutions are willing to build that kind of growth.

Every meaningful breakthrough in my life shared two ingredients.

Preparation that widened my capacity.

Trust that opened doors preparation alone could not reach.

I learned that hard work produces progress, but trust produces access.

People follow the person whose effort is steady and whose word can carry weight.

They invest in leaders who do not rush their rise, who build depth before display, and who keep commitments even when no one is watching.

When effort becomes consistent and trust becomes predictable, opportunities begin to behave differently.

Your work moves farther.

Your name travels ahead of you.

Your results start attracting people who believe in your discipline more than your ambition.

That is the moment when hustle stops being noisy and starts becoming strength.

It is the point where credibility multiplies your reach, and your preparation meets a reward that no shortcut can produce.

That is how leaders move from hoping for a chance to being trusted with responsibility that lasts.

THREE

PREPARED BY HUSTLE, PAID BY TRUST

The boy in the photograph looks confident. He is standing straight, shoulders back, wearing a blue shirt that has clearly seen better days. The smile is real, but it carries more determination than ease. That boy is me on matriculation day for my first degree, many years ago.

If you saw only that picture, you might assume the story behind it was one of hardship and limited means. That would not be true. I grew up in a stable home. My father served for many years as a senior economic adviser in government. He worked across several administrations from the 1980s onward and helped shape decisions that influenced the country's economic direction until he retired about fifteen years ago. My mother held a senior position in a government department comparable to the Department of Defense, then left to pursue her own ventures. We were not poor. We lived with structure, order, and opportunity.

Yet even with that background, I made a decision that changed the way my life unfolded. I chose to stand on my own. I wanted to learn what my abilities could carry without relying on family resources. That choice made the path harder, but it made the lessons deeper. Leadership often begins when you voluntarily accept weight you did not need to carry.

On that matriculation morning, there was no ceremony in the house, no crowd following me to campus. I stood in a small room, pressing a tired blue shirt that had already served more years than the fabric deserved. The collar was thin, the seams were worn, and the color had faded, but it was what I had chosen to wear. I pressed it until it held its shape and decided that my attitude would do the rest. You do not always control what you start with, but you can control the standard you bring to it.

Later, when I looked back at that photo, I understood what that season represented. It was not a picture of poverty. It was a picture of responsibility. I was stepping into my first degree in finance with a clear, self-imposed rule: no family funding and no student loans. The fees, the meals, the transport, and every small cost in between would be my duty. I was not trying to be heroic. I was trying to be accountable.

The way I chose finance was anything but strategic. One day at a bus stop, I asked a tutor what course he thought I should study. He said one word, "Finance," and that word set a direction for years of my life. There was no formal career guidance. There were no aptitude tests. Many people make major life choices exactly like that, on the strength of a passing suggestion. One quiet comment can turn into a decade of commitment.

My father supported my enrollment but did not pay the fees. My mother told me clearly that she would not contribute. I did not argue. I had already decided that this was my responsibility. When tuition was due, I found a way to meet it. When I could not pay on time, the university locked me out of class until the balance was cleared. I never owned a textbook for that degree. I took notes on loose sheets, folded them with care, and guarded them as if each page were a valuable document.

There was no private study room waiting for me at home. I studied wherever I could work. Many evenings ended in business centers where old computers sat in long rows. I paid for time in small blocks and watched the clock on the screen as closely as I watched the material I was studying. When the time expired, my session ended, not because the work was complete, but because I could not pay for one more minute. From the outside, my life looked like a string of small struggles. From the inside, it was training in concentration, discipline, and endurance.

Around that same period, I recognized something important. If I wanted to move beyond survival and begin to build something, I needed skills the syllabus did not offer. I had begun taking on small side businesses. I wanted to connect with companies, submit proposals, and win contracts, but I did not know how to write a proper business proposal. I was still a teenager, eager but inexperienced.

During a Communications in English class, I approached the lecturer and asked if he could teach us proposal writing. His answer was simple. It was not in the syllabus. That conversation stayed with me. Formal systems usually teach what is planned. Life demands what is necessary. No one was going to design a curriculum around the skills I needed to survive and grow. If I wanted those skills, I would have to go after them myself.

So I began to teach myself. I looked for examples of proposals wherever I could find them. I borrowed, observed, and studied the structure. I wrote rough drafts at night, corrected them, and improved each time I saw a better model. Each attempt felt awkward, but with every version I understood a little more. That process built more than writing ability. It taught me a permanent rule: you cannot wait for a system to hand you what your future requires.

To keep my education going, I turned every honest opportunity I could find into income. I helped people write and refine résumés. Some of them were classmates, others were older professionals who needed someone to present their experience clearly. Certain jobs paid, others did not, but every interaction sharpened my eye for detail and my listening skills. I spoke to employers, asked about openings, forwarded résumés when people trusted me to represent them, and answered simple questions when companies wanted to know more. I did not have a title for what I was doing. In reality, it was early recruitment and screening work.

I also connected buyers and sellers in small real estate deals and earned modest commissions. I encouraged people to subscribe to stock offerings and received small fractions of brokerage fees. None of these efforts made me rich, but they kept me in school. I was still a finance student on paper, but in practice I was learning sales, negotiation, communication, and entrepreneurship. When you treat small opportunities with respect, you train yourself for larger ones.

Those years were not the end of my education. They were the beginning of a pattern. Later in life, after I had completed an MBA that I paid for myself, I returned to earn a second undergraduate degree in Information Technology Management. This time I used federal aid and student loans, drawing on structures that had not been available or known to me during my first degree. The contrast mattered. My early education was funded by hustle. My later education combined experience with formal support. Both seasons taught different lessons about responsibility and growth.

In my second year of that first degree, the fatigue of constant work forced me to become more efficient. If I could not buy textbooks, I learned from people. I asked stronger students to explain concepts and then turned around and taught those same concepts to others. Teaching forced me to simplify ideas until they were clear. It became one of the most reliable ways I learned. When you can teach a subject clearly, you rarely forget it.

Even with all this effort, there came a point where small gains were not enough. Tuition still increased. Living costs did not shrink. The part-time hustles kept me afloat, but they did not move me forward at the pace I needed. I reached a point where continuing in the same way would only prolong the strain. At some stage in every career, the question changes from "How do I survive?" to "How do I step up?"

I decided to aim higher than my circumstances suggested. I prepared a business proposal for a multinational bank with a global presence. The bank operated in more than sixty countries, had its headquarters in London, and was led by a British chief executive. It was the kind of institution most students my age only read about in financial reports. My "company" at the time was a registered name and a folder of ideas written on borrowed paper. There was no office, no team, and no track record. What I had was a growing set of skills, hours of unpaid preparation, and the willingness to present value with seriousness.

Walking into that bank's office was a test of my own self-belief. The polished floors, the quiet corridors, and the confident pace of the people who worked there all carried a message. This was a place that dealt with scale and influence. I submitted the proposal expecting a polite rejection or, more likely, no response at all.

Instead, the bank approved the proposal in full and awarded the contract. They did more than that. They paid the entire amount upfront. Until that moment, every job I had done paid only after the work was complete, often after a long wait. Holding that check, I did not worry that the paper might disappear. I worried that the institution might change its mind, because I had never seen that level of trust placed in me before the work was finished.

I delayed cashing it until I had delivered. I needed to prove to myself that I could meet the standard the bank had assumed I could reach. That project was not only about revenue. It was about recognition. It confirmed something I had slowly been learning through each late night and each small job. People are often willing to believe in you when they see that you have already been acting as if the opportunity were yours.

That bank contract was my first major recruitment and services engagement with a global institution. It did not appear out of nowhere. It sat on top of years of small, unseen efforts: the résumés written for modest fees, the unpaid help offered to job seekers, the trial-and-error proposals, the real estate introductions, the phone calls to employers no one else dared to make. Hustle prepared the ground. Trust delivered the breakthrough.

In leadership, this pattern repeats itself more often than we admit. You work for years where no one seems to be watching. You solve problems in quiet places. You develop habits that do not have impressive titles attached to them. Then one decision-maker, one institution, or one opportunity appears and says, in effect, "We will pay you in advance. We believe you will deliver."

Prepared by hustle, paid by trust. That is how many real leaders are made.

Those early experiences became a private MBA in human behavior. I learned that competence earns respect and consistency earns belief. People may admire your skill, but they follow your reliability. Leaders rise when they become the person others can depend on when it matters.

Money was scarce during those years, so reputation became a form of currency. Every deadline met and every promise kept quietly lifted my credibility. I did not have the resources to advertise, so I earned visibility through performance. I did not have organizations championing my progress, so trust became my introduction. The same principle still governs the strongest teams and institutions. Credibility first, scale later.

There were moments of embarrassment too. I remember standing outside a classroom because tuition had not been paid. Friends walked past without saying a word. Pride wanted to disappear. Determination wanted to continue. Leadership often starts in the tension between those two impulses. You decide who you will be when the circumstances are unkind.

The memory of that worn blue shirt often returned to me. It reminded me that humility is a more dependable foundation than perfection. Each semester repeated a familiar cycle. Hustle, negotiate, fall behind, recover, and rebuild. Yet persistence compounds. The person who keeps moving eventually outruns the person who waits for ideal conditions.

Every workplace in America is filled with people replaying that same cycle in quiet ways. They balance responsibilities, carry private concerns, and show up even when confidence is thin. Leaders who remember their own early struggles manage such people differently. They set standards without losing empathy. They reward effort even before success reaches full strength. That difference separates those who command from those who influence.

At the height of those years, one evening at the business center shaped my approach to preparation. The room was busy and filled with noise. I was trying to format a proposal with software I barely knew. The attendant warned that my time was almost over. I asked for five more minutes, but he refused. The screen shut down mid-sentence.

Walking home, I replayed the minutes I had wasted. It would have been easy to blame the attendant or the system, but I chose a different response. I decided that next time I would work faster and prepare better. That night became a leadership rule I still follow. Improve what is within your control and refuse to surrender energy to anything else.

That simple discipline strengthens careers and organizations. Leaders who master it rarely complain because they understand where real leverage begins.

Over time, even the attendant at that business center changed his tone. I had become a regular. He started giving me quiet extensions, sometimes adding extra minutes without charge. People often reward consistency without being asked. Reliability creates invisible allies.

When the first bank contract arrived, I returned to that same place to complete the final documents. The familiar hum of the computers felt different that night. Every challenge had turned into capability. Every constraint had shaped endurance. Every small assignment had contributed to the confidence needed for larger opportunities.

Preparation had disguised itself as struggle.

That realization became my definition of leadership. You convert limitations into competence until competence earns trust. Once you see challenges through that lens, you stop waiting for permission to grow.

I often think of Roosevelt's words. Do what you can with what you have where you are. At that stage, I had scraps of paper, fatigue, and determination, yet they were enough to build momentum. Many professionals today are slowed by comparison. They wait for tools or titles. They wait for certainty. They wait for ideal timing. Leadership does not emerge from ideal conditions. It develops in necessary ones.

That principle guided me into the next test, which changed the direction of my career.

The day I entered that multinational bank stayed with me for years. The building communicated power. The hallways were quiet. The people moved with the confidence of those who believed they belonged. I held a proposal I created on borrowed computers and printed with money counted down to the last coin. My suit did not match, and my confidence almost didn't either.

Still, I had done the work. I understood the problem the bank faced, and I believed I could solve it. I did not have refined English or polished slides, but I had conviction. Conviction persuades even when vocabulary struggles to keep up.

When the bank's human resources department approved my proposal, I wondered if he had made an error. When the finance officer handed me a full payment in advance, I felt a weight heavier than celebration. It was the weight of trust. I placed the envelope in a drawer for days. I refused to cash it until the work was complete. I did not fear the check disappearing. I feared failing to honor the trust that had been placed in me.

The experience taught me that organizations do not always choose the most polished candidate. They often choose the one who speaks with clarity, follows through, and shows evidence of reliability. Confidence did not give me trust. Trust gave me confidence.

Months later, the bank held a recruitment event at a city auditorium. Their British CEO flew in and carried the room with a steady presence. When he acknowledged my work publicly, I felt humbled and strengthened at the same time. A boy who once wrote notes on scraps of paper now stood recognized by the leader of an international institution. His presence reminded me that leadership is not only about direction but affirmation. When leaders show up, others rise.

The recognition confirmed something simple. Trust multiplies progress. It shortens negotiation, reduces supervision, and fuels responsibility. Every strong institution depends on it.

When I eventually hired my own teams, I remembered that lesson. I looked for people who could be trusted when pressure was high. Skills attracted attention, but integrity sustained advancement. Hustle without character is movement without progress. Character turns out results into reputation.

Success did not feel like victory in those early years. It felt like responsibility. That first bank project made me cautious rather than triumphant. I double-checked every detail and reviewed every document. Insecurities often become early tutors. Over time, those habits turned into systems. Systems create consistency, and consistency creates freedom.

Credibility compounds like interest. Every promise kept enlarges your influence. Break one, and the balance resets. People who seem to rise quickly usually have years of deposits in private discipline and responsible effort.

During that period, I lived between contrasts. I executed projects for international banks during the day and negotiated for affordable meals at night. Progress became my only luxury. Each referral came from work done well, not advertising. Momentum replaced luck.

Younger students often asked how I managed. I told them the truth. Consistency becomes a greater advantage than brilliance when brilliance is inconsistent. Talent may open the door, but dependability keeps it open.

Organizations often forget this. They build hiring systems around degrees and technical skills and overlook reliability. The result is a widening leadership gap. America faces that same challenge today. The nation has talent but lacks trusted doers. Many gifted professionals hesitate until they feel ready. Many organizations promote those who look prepared rather than those who have learned to perform under real pressure.

Readiness is not a feeling. It is a decision proven through action. That global bank trusted me before I looked ready, and their trust forced me to meet a higher standard.

That experience shaped every negotiation that followed. I learned that people buy three things long before they buy a product. They buy belief in your competence. They buy clarity in your message. They buy alignment between what you say and what you do.

Lose any of the three and influence collapses. Keep them aligned and you can move institutions in any sector, including the ones struggling most in America today.

My blue shirt and scraps of paper had done their work. They built endurance, humility, and the strength to communicate value without embellishment. These qualities rarely appear on a résumé, yet they form the foundation of leadership. Too many professionals chase the appearance of success before building the substance of it. They invest in polish when they should invest in preparation.

The economy rewards preparedness. The workplace rewards reliability. Nations reward people who can be trusted to act. America's widening talent gap is not rooted in a lack of intelligence. It is rooted in the shortage of trusted leaders prepared to learn while leading.

The journey from scraps to signatures was never about material change. It was about psychological strength. It was about shifting from trying to prove worth into developing competence.

Every hardship carried a lesson. Mine built resilience. Mine strengthened persuasion. Convincing a global institution to believe in a student company required alignment between story and action. The same principle powers influence in every domain, from small teams to national leadership. People align with what they trust.

That first project closed a chapter but opened a philosophy. It taught me that progress is built through trust supported by disciplined effort. Titles fade. Trust remains.

Many young professionals tell me they are waiting for the right time. They believe the conditions must improve before they act. Conditions rarely improve first. People do. The moment you move, opportunities rearrange themselves around progress.

Even now, I keep a faded copy of that first proposal. The creases and handwritten corrections remind me that belief shapes possibility. A beginning made of scraps can still finance the future.

That idea extends far beyond personal ambition. It applies to nations. America is still full of bright minds waiting for an invitation to begin. The country's talent gap will close when more people learn to act with what they have and institutions learn to trust those who demonstrate readiness through responsibility.

Abraham Lincoln once said that preparation precedes opportunity. That principle carried me from obscurity to influence. It remains the path through which nations rebuild their leadership capacity.

Preparation. Opportunity. Trust. These three forces shape every chapter. They shaped mine. They will shape the leaders America needs next.

Persuasion – Alignment in Action

I learned persuasion long before I ever heard the term defined. My classroom was the sidewalk. The sun was high, the air was heavy, and the work was simple. I approached strangers and tried to convince them to subscribe to initial public offerings. There was no corporate badge on my chest, no promotional leaflet in my hand, and no budget to soften rejection. It was only my voice, my belief, and my willingness to hear a hundred rejections to earn a single agreement. That was where persuasion stopped being theory and became a necessity.

I discovered something essential in those moments. You can only communicate what you truly are. Persuasion does not begin with technique. It begins with identity. The real question is not what to say. The real question is who is speaking. What do you believe. What do you stand for. What do you consider non-negotiable. If your inner convictions are unsettled, your communication will be uncertain. Every form of influence begins with an internal sale. Until you accept your own value, no one else will.

I had many reasons to stop. Tuition was unpaid, textbooks were out of reach, and my path seemed unclear. Yet an internal belief quietly insisted that I had something worthwhile to offer. That belief opened doors that qualifications could not. Leaders face the same choice every day. Before you persuade others to share your vision, you must persuade yourself to stand inside it. Self-persuasion is the seed of every outward influence.

Some leaders talk endlessly about goals yet rarely move people. Others speak only briefly and create commitment that outlives policy. The difference is alignment. Strategy may impress, but alignment inspires. Compliance is temporary. Conviction is durable. Authority can instruct people to act, but persuasion turns that action into ownership.

Bill Gates described how, in his twenties, he focused completely on advancing software beyond what anyone expected. Competitors noticed his stamina before they noticed his intelligence. They saw the level of belief that could convince others through sheer certainty. That was his persuasive advantage.

My circumstances were different, but the engine was the same. I had no product, no brand, no platform. What I had was hunger. Hunger persuades in ways resources cannot. Every rejection on the street forced me to refine my message. Every uncertain response developed patience. Every small success confirmed that conviction can multiply faster than capital.

Persuasion is not magic. It is method. It follows a sequence anyone can use. First you listen. Then you align. Then you clarify. Listening builds understanding. Alignment turns that understanding into shared purpose. Clarity turns shared purpose into language others can repeat. Omit any part of that sequence and persuasion collapses into noise.

Influence happens three times in order. First you persuade yourself. Then you persuade your team. Finally you persuade your stakeholders. The order matters. When you skip the first, the rest becomes performance. When you skip the second, the mission loses strength. When you skip the third, good ideas never leave the room.

Organizations that ignore this pattern face predictable consequences. Research firms continue to show that most transformation programs fail because leaders never win buy-in. When Gallup estimates that disengaged employees drain trillions from the American economy, the issue is not laziness. It is a signal that leadership communication has collapsed. Employees hear instructions without feeling conviction. They understand tasks without seeing purpose.

Every disengaged employee is a quiet review of leadership clarity. Persuasion fills that gap. It is the connection between direction and devotion.

There are examples across history. Kodak invented the digital camera yet persuaded itself that the future would resemble the past. Profit preserved loyalty to film. The result was structural collapse. Wells Fargo focused so heavily on sales targets that persuasion was replaced with pressure. A culture meant to motivate turned into one that violated trust. The penalties reached the billions.

Then consider Steve Jobs launching the iPod using only seven words. One thousand songs in your pocket. He did not describe circuits or storage. He described freedom. That sentence persuaded millions because it aligned technology with personal desire. Toyota accomplished something similar when it convinced the world that quality, not appearance, defined excellence. Every vehicle became a visible promise. That is persuasion expressed through alignment.

Persuasion looks simple but it is not easy. Spend most of your effort listening and the rest speaking. The better you listen, the less you will need to talk. If your team cannot repeat your message in a single sentence, you have spoken too much and communicated too little. Real persuasion is proven when people echo your words as if they originated with them.

This principle applies everywhere. It applies in classrooms, corporate offices, government halls, small businesses, and national conversations. Persuasion is the unseen structure beneath progress. Without it, competence sits unused.

Singapore demonstrated this when its early leaders convinced the population that survival would require discipline and shared sacrifice. They aligned national goals with personal dignity. That alignment transformed compliance into pride. The nation rose into one of the most competitive economies in the world. The same citizens who once resisted limits eventually embraced them because persuasion made the purpose personal. Transformation follows persuasion. Decline follows its absence.

Persuasion also requires stamina. Influence weakens when endurance fades. You must persuade yourself again and again, especially when confidence drops or fatigue builds. The internal voice must stay stronger than external resistance. Words create intention but consistency creates credibility. When actions match declarations, persuasion becomes trust.

My challenges were never with people who refused to help. My challenge was ignorance, both mine and theirs. I had to outlearn my limitations. That is why I began reading multiple books at the same time. The goal was not speed. It was synthesis. Knowledge became my competitive advantage. Hustle opened doors. Preparation kept them from closing.

Knowledge strengthens persuasion because knowledge strengthens empathy. The more you learn, the more accurately you can understand what matters to others. Reading broadens perspective, not just information. Every effective persuader studies the people they hope to move before trying to move them.

Persuasion also invites isolation. When you decide to stand for something original, you will grow apart from those who prefer imitation. Many want agreement, not challenge. Leadership is lonely long before it becomes visible. That loneliness examines your conviction. Can you speak when no one agrees. Can you remain steady when applause is absent. Persuasion grows in silence. You refine your voice privately before you use it publicly.

And yet, persuasion shapes every corner of American life. It influences whether individuals advance or stall, whether teams unite or divide, whether companies innovate or remain stuck, and whether the nation can rebuild a leadership culture strong enough to close the talent gap. Technology may accelerate change, but persuasion determines participation. Leaders must convince employees to learn new skills, customers to adapt, and communities to believe. Those who master persuasion will shape the future. Those who ignore it will be shaped by it.

The rule remains the same whether on a street corner or in a boardroom. Alignment must come before action. People will not commit until they see their reflection in your mission. Persuasion at its best is not manipulation. It is synchronization. It is the joining of motives in a way that turns shared interest into shared movement.

That understanding did not come from textbooks. It came from years of hustling for opportunity and earning trust one conversation at a time. It took me from sidewalks to boardrooms. Hustle prepared me. Trust rewarded me. Persuasion scaled both.

When the bank paid me in full before I delivered the work, they were responding not to appearance but to conviction. Persuasion had already done the heavy lifting. It translated belief into trust and trust into opportunity.

That remains the sequence that builds influence. Persuasion produces trust. Trust sustains leadership.

The more I advanced, the clearer one truth became. Persuasion is the quiet structure beneath every visible success. It builds teams, secures investors, restores confidence, and moves institutions long after formal authority runs out. Many leaders confuse persuasion with performance. They mistake charisma for credibility. Real influence is measured not by applause during a meeting but by alignment after it.

I have seen senior executives lose entire divisions because they could not connect their strategies to human meaning. They spoke in numbers instead of purpose. Charts explain what to do. Conviction explains why it matters. Until the why is owned, the how remains fragile.

When I began leading teams of my own, I learned that persuasion does not mean convincing people to think like you. Persuasion means creating a setting where they can see their success inside your vision. Once that happens, action becomes momentum.

This is the cost of leadership in a country facing a talent shortage. The United States does not lack smart people. It lacks aligned people. Persuasion creates that alignment.

Persistence and preparation bring persuasion to life. Improvisation fades and rarely scales. Before every presentation, I researched the audience. I studied what they feared losing and what they hoped to gain. Most decisions are driven by preservation before ambition. Address the first and you earn attention. Address the second and you earn commitment.

Every audience has a currency. Some respond to data. Some respond to stories. Some respond to trust. Persuasion begins when you identify that currency and speak in it without abandoning authenticity.

Early in my career, I believed information alone persuaded people. Over time, I learned that clarity carries greater power. The more I simplified my message, the faster people agreed. Simplicity respects the listener. Simplicity builds trust. Trust creates movement.

Silence also has persuasive strength. Every negotiation has a moment when the right move is to stop speaking. When you fill silence with nervous explanations, you reduce your authority. When you hold silence with composure, you increase it. Composure is a form of content.

Persuasion weakens when ego grows. The moment your desire to be right becomes stronger than your desire to align, communication turns into conflict. The goal of persuasion is not to win arguments. The goal is to win understanding.

Information supports persuasion. Emotion accelerates it. The best persuaders combine both. Evidence calms the mind. Empathy opens it. The balance is intentional.

I saw this during a negotiation when a client considered canceling a project due to rising costs. Spreadsheets proved the value, but they didn't move the decision. I closed the laptop and shared the story of the first contract that changed my life. A stranger believed in a young student and paid in full before delivery. That story brought meaning to the numbers. The client renewed the agreement. Logic supported the decision. Story secured it.

Storytelling remains persuasion's oldest tool because it mirrors how the mind remembers. Facts inform. Stories endure.

***

Persuasion is also an ethical test. The more capable you become, the easier it is to misuse. True persuasion lifts people; manipulation uses them. Intent draws the line. When both sides gain, influence becomes leadership. When only one side gains, influence becomes coercion. I gave myself a rule early: never promise what I could not deliver. A short win bought through exaggeration destroys long-term trust, and one broken promise erases the power of many fulfilled ones. The same principle governs nations, institutions, and relationships. Credibility always compounds, and deception always reverses it.

When digital communication became the dominant tool in business, many assumed persuasion would become easier. They believed reach would replace relevance. But sending messages is not the same as being understood. Technology can deliver words quickly; it cannot add weight to them. Alignment still does the heavy lifting. Every era returns to the same fundamentals: listen carefully, speak clearly, act consistently. These behaviors outlast every platform. They turn managers into leaders people rely on.

I learned this again while advising a financial client that was struggling with internal resistance. Their employees had grown tired of announcements. I asked the executives to pause directives for one month and replace every statement with a question. They were hesitant, but they tried. Within weeks, morale shifted. Listening did what memos could not. The persuasion they needed was not toward customers but toward their own people. Many American companies face the same gap today. Employees understand tasks, but not purpose. They hear instructions, but not conviction. That divide drains engagement and weakens performance.

Persuasion must begin at the top, but it must also be felt at the bottom. The strongest organizations build alignment into their culture. They ensure that every policy, meeting, and product answers the same question: How does this serve the mission we share? When that clarity is missing, confusion grows. When that clarity is present, bureaucracy becomes coordination instead of obstruction.

This applies far beyond corporate settings. Parents use persuasion to guide children. Teachers use it to shape minds. Nations use it to renew confidence in institutions. The sequence never changes. Empathy first. Alignment second. Clarity third. When leaders follow that sequence, even complicated goals gain momentum.

Mental stamina supports all of it. Influence falters when endurance collapses. There were days when nothing worked— clients canceled, opportunities evaporated, and momentum stalled. Those were the moments when persuasion became internal work. I reminded myself that perseverance itself persuades. The person who refuses to quit eventually shapes the narrative of their environment. Hustle trained me for persuasion. Trust validated it. Every contract afterward followed the same pattern: belief shaping alignment, alignment producing trust, trust producing results.

Over time, I saw that persuasion and leadership are inseparable. One is the method; the other is the outcome. Leadership falters the moment persuasion stops. You cannot lead change if you cannot align interests. That reality affects families, companies, and countries. Alignment is not about universal agreement; it is about shared direction. Consensus produces polite meetings; alignment produces measurable progress.

That is why every aspiring leader must practice persuasion in daily life. The goal is not eloquence; the goal is clarity. When you become clear, people become confident.

***

When I teach persuasion now, I summarize it in five sentences:
Believe before you speak.
Listen before you advise.
Simplify before you amplify.
Clarify before you close.
Align before you act.

These lines compress years of work into principles anyone can use. Persuasion delayed is leadership delayed. The longer a leader postpones a needed conversation, the longer confusion undermines progress. Speed of persuasion often decides speed of performance.

In today's economy, persuasion is no longer optional. It is infrastructure. Artificial intelligence can process information, but it cannot create belief. Automation can complete tasks, but it cannot inspire alignment. As the country grapples with rapid change—skills gaps, workforce shortages, institutional distrust—persuasion becomes the cornerstone of national renewal. The leaders who will guide America forward will not be those with the loudest voices, but those who can align teams, communities, and institutions around a clear purpose.

My own life illustrates this truth. Hustle opened the first door. Trust kept it open. Persuasion expanded the room. Every major advancement in my career can be traced to a moment when what I offered aligned with what another person valued. That alignment created opportunity.

And so persuasion concludes where negotiation begins. One builds belief; the other protects respect. Persuasion earns trust; negotiation sustains it. The next principle extends the journey that started with hustle, sharpened through preparation, and proven through trust.

Negotiation – Protecting Value Without Burning Bridges

Real estate became one of my earliest and most demanding classrooms. I did not own property, licenses, or an office. I was simply the link between people who wanted something and people who had it. I found buyers, approached sellers, and relied on the credibility of senior brokers who allowed me to speak on their behalf. The commissions were small, but the lessons were lasting. Every conversation felt like walking a tightrope. If I pushed too hard, the deal collapsed. If I yielded too quickly, I lost value I could not afford to lose. Those moments formed my first lessons in negotiation.

Hustle had kept me moving. Persuasion had helped me connect. Negotiation taught me how to protect what I had earned.

Negotiation is not a contest of power. It is the discipline of holding your value while preserving someone else's dignity. Many leaders never learn that balance. Some push so forcefully that they damage the relationship. Others surrender so quickly that they weaken respect. Both choices cost more than they appear to.

Every sector shows the same pattern. Partnerships fall apart because expectations were never clarified. Customers leave because the promise was not stated plainly. Teams disengage because leaders never learned how to disagree without causing harm. Most failures that appear sudden usually began as small negotiation errors. Someone assumed clarity where none existed.

Some people treat negotiation like combat. They win the moment and lose the future. Others treat it as charity and give away terms that their teams will later regret. Strong negotiators do neither. They think in cycles, not events. They aim for continuity, not applause. They defend value without damaging trust and leave the door open for the next conversation.

I learned this through painful experience. After brokering a promising property sale, I discovered that a senior broker had written terms that excluded me from the agreement. It was not illegal. It was simply unfair. I had a choice. Become bitter or become better. I chose the latter. That loss forced me to put every understanding in writing. It taught me that trust is a measurable asset and that clarity protects everyone at the table.

Every negotiation balances three elements: time, trust, and terms.

Time determines leverage. People who prepare early rarely panic late.

Trust determines tone. When people believe your word, they open cooperation instead of defense.

Terms determine clarity. Clear terms prevent resentful agreements that unravel later.

Before each negotiation, I learned to ask myself three questions.

What is my real value in this situation?
What is their real value?
How can both sides walk away with dignity?

Those three questions changed everything. They aligned my motives with a long-term view. They turned negotiation from a tug-of-war into a conversation about continuity.

Years later, the same principles played out on an international stage. Some companies entered new markets with force instead of diplomacy. They moved fast, ignored local realities, and assumed momentum would erase resistance. It did not. Cities pushed back. Regulators reacted. Billions were lost, not because of weak ideas, but because of weak negotiation.

Other companies took the opposite path. After facing major setbacks, they listened, rebuilt relationships, and changed posture. That shift created decades of stability. Influence grows when humility enters the room.

Before any negotiation, preparation remained my foundation. Confidence cannot be improvised. I studied what the other side valued, what they feared losing, and what they considered fair. The more informed I was, the calmer I became. Calmness shapes the outcome. People trust the person who stays composed when pressure rises.

Negotiation is emotional before it is logical. Facts frame decisions, but feelings move them. When tension rises, logic evaporates. Skilled negotiators regulate temperature. They acknowledge concerns without surrendering value.

I remember watching seasoned brokers in those early years. They managed tone more skillfully than they managed price. They smiled when others frowned. They stayed quiet when others raised their voices. They paused at the right moment. Composure gave them an advantage that no script could replace.

Dialogue builds the middle ground. True dialogue is listening in motion. People reveal more through pauses and tone than through formal statements. During one negotiation, a buyer insisted that his offer was final. Yet each time I mentioned speed of delivery, his voice softened. That was the hinge. I offered a faster timeline rather than a lower price. He agreed within minutes. The lesson stayed. People rarely need the cheapest offer. They need the most aligned one.

Settlement is the final step. It is where talk becomes structure. The best outcome is not one where you take everything. It is one where both sides leave with respect intact. Satisfaction comes and goes. Respect remains. I began using one test before signing anything. Would I want to work with this person again. If the answer was no, the deal was incomplete.

Negotiation exposes character. Delay reveals temperament. Anyone can appear ethical when the outcome is certain. Patience during uncertainty separates the trustworthy from the tactical.

Over time, patterns became clear. Some people negotiate to dominate. They win noise and lose networks. Some negotiate for peace. They lose respect and revenue. Some negotiate for immediate gain. They chase margin but not loyalty. Strong leaders negotiate for continuity. They think beyond the moment and protect the future while securing the present.

When I entered management and later consulting, those early lessons returned. Whether discussing client contracts, vendor agreements, or partnership renewals, the same three forces appeared. Preparation shaped leverage. Listening discovered alignment. Clarity preserved respect.

Negotiation became the quiet difference between people who earn income and people who earn loyalty. It remains one of the most practical tools for any leader who hopes to close America's leadership gap. Our workforce suffers not only from lack of skill but from lack of people who can resolve conflict without destroying cooperation. Nations rise when their leaders know how to protect value while keeping bridges open.

Great negotiation turns tension into progress and disagreement into partnership. That skill is not a bonus for leaders. It is a requirement.

The Language of Gesture

Negotiation rarely begins with words. It begins when you walk into the room. People notice how you stand, how you shake hands, how you look at them, long before they process your argument. Years before I sat in American boardrooms, I learned this in a quiet office many miles away, in a meeting that changed the arc of my consulting work.

By that time, I had advised several banks and insurance companies. The largest insurer in the country wanted my help, but we never aligned. If the issue was not pricing, it was exclusivity. Nearly every major client demanded that I work only for them. Others wanted me to ignore poor service in the name of profit. I was not willing to attach my name to a brand that mistreated customers. Values mattered more than invoices.

One morning my phone rang. The number was unfamiliar. The caller introduced himself as the head of a division at a new insurance company backed by a firm based in London with nearly two centuries of history and offices in South and West Africa. They had studied the market, seen my work, and reached the same conclusion: for this kind of project, I was the person to call. They asked if I would visit their office.

When I arrived, I did not begin with a pitch. I began with presence. I greeted each person in the room, sat upright, listened more than I spoke, and let my body say what my résumé did not need to repeat. The head of division was relaxed, open, and curious. We spent an hour in what was supposed to be a hard negotiation that turned into an honest conversation about the industry, the gaps in customer experience, and the kind of company they wanted to build. We were not trading lines; we were reading each other's posture.

At the end of the meeting, he asked for my fee. I quoted the highest rate I had ever named in that category of work. He did not flinch. He simply said yes. No counteroffer, no posturing. The decision was not based on a slide deck. It flowed from alignment, and that alignment had been communicated as much through tone and gesture as through words. Presence had done half the work before pricing ever appeared.

That agreement grew into a long relationship. We moved into other product lines. Their numbers rose, customer adoption increased, and the company became the preferred choice for the everyday insurance buyer. My phone began to ring with competitors asking when the contract would expire so they could hire me. I declined. Loyalty and shared values were worth more than a higher fee. The deal had started as a business conversation. It became a partnership because our gestures and decisions matched the story we told about ourselves.

Gesture is the first negotiation. It decides whether people believe what you say before you finish saying it.

Everywhere I have worked, from small firms to global companies, the pattern is the same. People listen with their eyes first. A leader says the right things about respect and inclusion but never looks up from a laptop when staff speak. A manager talks about "open doors" while standing with arms folded and shoulders tense. Employees remember the posture, not the policy.

In the United States, this gap shows up in a thousand quiet ways. Executives speak about culture, yet their body language signals impatience. Public officials talk about service, yet their faces broadcast disdain. Parents urge children to be confident while shrinking in their own interactions. The message and the gesture do not match, and the next generation learns to distrust both.

America does not suffer from a shortage of training material. It suffers from leaders whose presence contradicts their message.

That is one reason the talent gap widens. People are reluctant to follow those whose eyes say "leave" while their words say "stay."

Leadership presence begins with physical honesty. When you walk into a room standing tall, making steady eye contact, and listening without distraction, you tell people they matter before you speak a single sentence. When you slow your breathing, lower your shoulders, and give your full attention, you create space where others feel safe to contribute. In that space, talent emerges.

Presence is not a performance. It is alignment. The body reflects what the mind believes.

I have sat through meetings where the presentation was flawless and the message was right, yet the room stayed cold. The leader spoke about collaboration while sitting apart from everyone else. He kept glancing at his watch, shifting in his chair, sending a steady stream of signals that said, "This is not important." Later he wondered why his team looked disengaged. They had listened carefully. They simply believed his posture more than his slide deck.

The same thing happens in American companies every day. Policies promise development, but leaders' gestures broadcast distance. We tell young professionals that they are "future leaders" while stepping back from them in conversation, cutting them off mid-sentence, or answering our phones while they speak. Those micro-moments train people to withdraw. They stop bringing ideas. They stop stretching. Eventually, they stop staying. The talent gap is not only a pipeline problem; it is often a presence problem.

Gesture is culture made visible. A company can print values on the wall, but employees read values from the way their leaders stand, listen, and respond under stress. Nations do the same. Citizens watch how public officials behave when they think no one is watching. Children study how adults carry themselves when decisions are hard. In time, gesture writes a story that no speech can erase.

For anyone who wants to lead, gesture is not a soft skill. It is a strategic one. When your words and your body move in the same direction, you increase trust without saying more. When they move in different directions, people quietly step back.

You can train this. Record yourself in a meeting. Do not listen for content the first time. Watch your posture, your eyes, your hands. Ask a trusted colleague, "How did you feel in my presence, not just what did you hear?" The answers may surprise you. Then adjust one habit at a time. Sit among your team instead of apart. Put the phone away. Hold eye contact long enough to show you are present. Smile when you agree. Stay calm when you disagree. These simple adjustments change more outcomes than an extra paragraph in your speech.

Strong leaders in any country, especially in a restless and gifted nation like the United States, cannot afford signals that confuse the people they hope to guide. If America wants to close its leadership gap, it will require more than new programs. It will require visible examples of men and women whose gestures and decisions match their words, day after day.

As my own work expanded, I came to see leadership as a choreography of small, consistent gestures. The way you enter a room. The way you greet the most junior person. The way you sit when someone disagrees. Each movement either supports or weakens your message. Hustle had taught me to speak up. Maturity taught me to let my presence do as much work as my words.

The language of gesture prepares every serious conversation that follows. It sets the stage for trust or doubt before the first offer appears. And even when leaders understand this, many still fall into subtle habits that slowly undermine their credibility. They are not dramatic failures. They are small patterns—tone, timing, fatigue, ego—that quietly erode alignment.

Those patterns are the silent killers of negotiation. They ruin more agreements than open conflict ever does.

The Silent Killers of Negotiation

There are forces that destroy negotiation long before a competitor arrives. They move quietly inside leaders and institutions and drain strength from the inside out. Four of them appear again and again in every industry and every sector. They are complacency, bureaucracy, arrogance, and slowness to adjust. They do not come with alarms. They arrive as comfort, habit, pride, and delay.

In corporate offices, government agencies, and small businesses across America, these four forces are doing more damage than any external rival. They block decisions, waste talent, and stall careers. They create the conditions that leave promising people unready to lead, even when they hold impressive titles. In a country that depends on initiative and innovation, these silent killers are a direct threat to the talent pipeline.

Complacency is the most attractive of the four because it feels like safety. A leader looks at last year's numbers and decides that the same approach will be enough next year. Teams that once fought hard for every sale begin to assume that customers will always return. Executives stop asking hard questions because past success feels like proof that nothing serious will change.

I saw this early in my consulting work. A client told me with complete confidence that they did not need to try anything new because profits were still strong. Six months later a competitor launched a new product and captured a large share of their market. They did not lose because they lacked resources. They lost because they trusted yesterday more than they studied today.

Complacency does not always look lazy. It often looks busy. The calendar stays full, meetings continue, and reports are produced. The real problem lies beneath the activity. The organization is no longer hungry. The same pattern plays out in careers. A professional reaches a certain level and stops learning. Promotions slow. Frustration rises. The world moves past them while they defend routines that no longer fit.

The only cure for complacency is honest curiosity. Leaders who keep asking what has changed, who is catching up, and what their people still need to learn rarely drift. They negotiate from current reality, not from memory of former victories.

Bureaucracy is complacency dressed in formal clothes. Systems that were once created to speed decisions begin to slow them. Forms multiply. Approvals pile up. Decisions that could be settled in one meeting now take months. Opportunity walks away while paperwork travels between desks.

In negotiation, bureaucracy sends a message you never want to send. It tells the other side that you cannot decide. It tells high potential employees that their ideas will wait in line behind procedure. It tells young talent that initiative will be punished with delay.

I remember speaking with a manager who had designed a faster way to onboard customers. His approach could have reduced cost and improved experience. His plan sat in internal review for eight months. By the time senior leaders looked at it, competitors had already acted. His idea was not rejected. It simply expired.

In a country that claims to value innovation, bureaucracy is one of the main reasons many bright Americans feel stuck. Talented people leave not because they lack loyalty but because they can no longer justify waiting.

The answer is empowerment. When capable people are trusted to decide within clear boundaries, negotiation gains speed. Customers feel it. Partners feel it. Employees feel it. Empowered teams move at the pace of relevance.

Arrogance is quieter but more dangerous. It appears when leaders begin to believe that their position guarantees their importance. Past success is treated as proof of permanent superiority. Instead of listening, they lecture. Instead of asking, they assume.

I once observed discussions between two large firms that were considering a merger. One senior executive dominated every conversation. He corrected his counterpart in public, quoted his company's revenue again and again, and dismissed concerns from his own team. By the second day, the other side had emotionally left the room. The deal eventually collapsed. On paper, the numbers made sense. In practice, the posture killed it.

Arrogance does not only damage large deals. It suffocates truth inside organizations. Employees stop bringing warnings because they know they will be ignored. Younger leaders stop offering ideas because they do not want to be embarrassed. Clients stop complaining because they assume nothing will change. On the surface, everything looks calm. Underneath, trust is draining away.

The antidote is humility combined with competence. Humility keeps a leader listening. Competence ensures that when they act, they act well. In negotiation, a humble question often creates more leverage than a proud statement. People open up to leaders who are confident enough to keep learning.

Slowness to adjust is usually the final stage. Complacency removes urgency. Bureaucracy slows decisions. Arrogance rejects feedback. The result is delay. The market changes, technology advances, and customers shift their expectations while leadership clings to old assumptions.

The story has repeated itself in many American companies. Well known brands that once dominated their industries hesitated when digital models appeared. Video rental stores watched streaming grow. Retailers watched online platforms expand. Banks watched fintech companies reimagine basic services. By the time many of them responded, the negotiation was over. Customers had already moved.

On a personal level, the same pattern shows up in careers. Professionals see new skills emerging but delay learning them. They hear about automation but assume their role will be exempt. They resist change until change removes their seat. At that point, adjustment is no longer a choice. It is a reaction.

Adaptability is now a core leadership skill in America. Leaders who recognize change early and engage it directly hold the advantage at the table. They can negotiate new partnerships, new models, and new roles for their people while there is still time to shape the terms.

These four killers rarely operate alone. Complacency makes leaders feel comfortable. Bureaucracy wraps that comfort in process. Arrogance tells them they are too important to be replaced. Slowness to adjust completes the cycle. The organization is still moving, but it is no longer moving in step with reality.

The danger is that each one feels reasonable while it is doing damage. Complacency feels like confidence. Bureaucracy feels like control. Arrogance feels like strength. Delay feels like caution. By the time results expose the truth, talent has left, customers have shifted, and public trust has faded.

I have seen this pattern in corporations, in nonprofits, in schools, and in government offices. I have also seen it in individuals who once had enormous promise. It is one of the reasons America has so many bright people who are still unready to lead at higher levels. They are capable, but they are trapped inside systems and habits that punish urgency, curiosity, and humility.

Breaking the pattern begins with self negotiation. Every leader, at every level, must ask hard questions. Am I still curious. Have I started to hide behind process. Am I listening less than I used to. Am I moving as fast as the world around me. Honest answers reveal whether these killers are already at work.

The enemy of progress is not failure. Failure teaches. The true enemy is drift that feels like success.

The modern world will not slow down for anyone. Technology will not wait for approval cycles. Global competition will not pause while leaders debate what to do next. Young professionals will not remain in places where effort and ideas are consistently delayed.

To stay relevant, leaders must replace complacency with curiosity, bureaucracy with empowerment, arrogance with humility, and slowness to adjust with thoughtful speed. These are not slogans. They are survival habits for any person or institution that wants to remain useful in the United States and beyond.

Hustle taught me to move. Trust taught me to move wisely. Together they formed a shield against these silent killers. They kept me alert when comfort tried to settle in.

Every negotiation, whether with a client, a board, a team, or a community, demands the same combination. You protect value by staying awake. You protect people by staying humble. You protect the future by moving when others prefer to wait.

No leader escapes storms. Plans fail. Deals fall through. Supporters grow quiet. In those moments, the leaders who survive are not the ones who felt most comfortable. They are the ones who trained themselves to keep going when comfort vanished. That is where the next discipline begins.

Resilience in the Storm

The emotional side of negotiation cannot be avoided. Leaders walk into high-stakes conversations carrying weight, fear, and doubt. What separates those who move forward from those who stall is not the absence of emotion but the speed of recovery. Mental stamina is not a gift. It is built through work, repetition, and discipline.

Novak Djokovic, one of the greatest competitors in tennis, once said that the biggest battle is never across the net. It is inside. He admits to feeling anger, doubt, and frustration. The difference is how long he stays there. Champions acknowledge what they feel, release it, and reset with focus. They use breathing, routines, and simple mental cues to return to the present point. The doubts still come, but they do not stay in charge.

Negotiation works the same way. A leader who clings to frustration loses clarity. A leader who pretends not to feel anything builds resentment that surfaces later in tone and decision. The strongest leaders acknowledge the strain, reset their focus, and return to the table with composure. Hustle trained me in that discipline. I could not afford to spend days in discouragement. Tuition still had to be paid. Clients still had to be found. Each setback forced me to release disappointment and return faster. Over time, that quick return became a habit. That habit was resilience.

People notice how you carry yourself when things are not going your way. They trust the leader who steadies quickly, who regains balance even while the problem is still unresolved. It is not brilliance alone that earns greater responsibility. It is composure under strain.

Every negotiation has its own weather. Some meetings feel calm. Others feel heated. Some turn without warning. You cannot control that climate, but you can control your response. Emotional management is not denial. It is direction. It is knowing when to pause, when to push, and when to pivot.

I learned this early in business. A client once raised his voice in anger, convinced that I had underdelivered. My first instinct was to defend myself and match his tone. Instead, I paused, took a slow breath, and said, "Tell me exactly what is not working, and let us fix it." The conversation changed in seconds. He apologized later and admitted that my calm response had forced him to look at the facts. That day I realized a simple rule. In every argument, someone has to calm down first. The one who does that usually wins the outcome that matters.

Resilience does not mean you never feel anger or fear. It means you recover faster than most people expect.

Emotional endurance often decides how far a career goes. In every field, you will meet people with similar intelligence and skill. Only a few rise into sustained leadership. The difference is often emotional elasticity, the ability to bounce back after rejection, mistakes, or criticism.

Resilience can be learned, but only through friction. It grows through failure, correction, and honest feedback. Reading about pressure points never toughens anyone. Living through them does. The ability to regain control during hard moments transforms not only your results but also how others see you. When teams watch their leader steady in the middle of chaos, their own confidence rises. Stability is contagious.

I once advised an executive whose quarterly results had fallen short. Shareholders were angry. The room was tense. He did not blame the market or his staff. He acknowledged the miss, accepted responsibility, and walked everyone through a clear plan to recover. His tone was calm. His posture was firm. Afterward, one shareholder told me, "We are unhappy with the numbers, but we still believe in him." That is the invisible dividend of composure.

Resilience begins where excuses end. The moment you stop blaming circumstances, you start building control. Leaders who always look outward stay reactive. Leaders who accept responsibility stay proactive.

When demands rise, you have three practical choices. You can panic, you can pause, or you can plan. Panic drains energy. Pause restores balance. Planning restores direction. Leaders who learn to pause first recover faster. That brief pause, the mental gap between reaction and response, is where resilience starts.

Every difficult conversation and every setback gives you a chance to practice that pause. I trained it deliberately. When something went wrong, I asked one simple question: What can I still control? That question brought order back into the moment. Control what you can, release what you cannot. Over time, that mindset became an anchor.

Many organizations in the United States talk about burnout as if it were an outside force. In reality, burnout is what happens inside when stress piles up without recovery. It is the storm that grows because leaders never reset between challenges. The answer is not to glorify toughness. The answer is planned renewal.

Resilient people schedule recovery as seriously as results. They build habits that restore them: quiet reflection, physical exercise, spiritual or personal time, gratitude, simple moments with the people who matter. These are not luxuries. They are maintenance for leadership. Mental fatigue silently erodes negotiation strength. No one makes wise decisions from a state of chronic exhaustion that is pretending to be productivity.

I have watched capable executives make poor choices simply because they were tired. Fatigue distorts judgment. It enlarges threats and shrinks options. The leader who learns to rest before they break keeps an advantage. Hustle creates opportunity. Rest protects it.

Resilience also requires emotional honesty. Pretending to be unaffected does not make you strong. It makes you brittle. When leaders hide what they feel instead of processing it, the tension leaks into sarcasm, sharp emails, and sudden withdrawals. Hidden emotion does not disappear. It moves.

A senior manager once told me her team saw her as unpredictable. Some days she was supportive. Other days she was distant and hard. In private she admitted she was under heavy strain but did not want to show weakness. I told her, "Your team already knows something is wrong. They just do not know what it is." When she began to name her stress in simple, calm terms, the mood changed. Her honesty reduced the fear in the room. Her vulnerability did not weaken her authority. It stabilized it.

Controlled openness strengthens resilience. When people watch you fall, recover, and continue, they learn that failure is survivable. They become braver because you showed them how to stand up, not how to pretend you never fell.

Sports psychologists call this an emotional reset. Every serious athlete practices it. Missed points and bad calls must be released or they destroy the next play. Leadership follows the same rule. You will lose deals. You will face criticism. You will experience unfairness at times. What matters is how quickly you move from reaction back to focus.

In negotiation, that reset often decides whether a deal is saved or lost. If anger drives you, your words will work against you. If composure leads you, clarity follows. Emotional balance is one of the few skills you can carry into every setting.

During a contract discussion, a partner once grew aggressive over price. I felt irritation rise. Then I reminded myself of a simple truth. Emotion is always a form of leverage. Either it controls you, or you manage it. I lowered my tone, slowed my speech, and let silence do some of the work. Within minutes, the intensity faded. We closed the deal, not because I out-argued him, but because I outlasted my own frustration.

Resilience, at its core, is the discipline of staying useful while you are uncomfortable.

The same principle governs life outside of work. Every setback brings two battles. One is the external problem. The other is the internal reaction. You solve the first with strategy and effort. You master the second with patience. People often overestimate the power of plans and underestimate the power of steadiness.

In the storms of leadership, resilience is both shield and compass. It protects your clarity and directs your next move. Without it, intelligence becomes fragile and experience loses its value.

Hustle gave me resilience through necessity. Each rejection, each delayed payment, each disappointment stretched my capacity a little further. Trust refined that capacity into calm strength. Over time, what once shook me became familiar terrain.

Resilience is not glamorous. Most of the time it looks like quiet work. It is getting up on the days when nothing feels exciting. It is sending one more proposal after a string of refusals. It is listening carefully when you would rather withdraw. It is the decision to move forward without applause.

I remember a season when a client defaulted on a payment that could have carried my entire operation. Anger and disbelief came first. For a few hours, I let myself feel both. Then I sat down, wrote out a plan for new outreach, and started again. Within two weeks, the loss had turned into a lesson. The revenue mattered. The recovery mattered more. I learned that pain handled quickly becomes wisdom. Pain held too long becomes waste.

Emotional recovery is like muscle recovery. It needs repetition, rest, and awareness. Each cycle of stress can either weaken you or enlarge you, depending on how you move through it. Leaders who avoid all stress never grow. Leaders who engage it and then recover become stronger.

When I speak with executives about negotiation fatigue, I ask them how many important decisions they can make at their best before emotion begins to cloud their thinking. Most give a number that is too high. The mind, like the body, tires with overuse. Resilience depends less on how long you can push and more on how well you recover between pushes.

That is why elite competitors follow strict routines for recovery. They eat well. They rest. They review. Leadership requires the same discipline. After intense discussions, pause on purpose. Review what happened. Draw out one or two lessons. Then let the event go. Carrying emotional residue from one meeting into the next is how burnout begins.

Resilience is also strategic. It keeps movement alive when conditions are not friendly. In times of disruption, I have watched two groups of organizations in America. One group freezes and waits for certainty. The other group adapts in motion. The second group survives more often. Their resilience is not luck. It is preparation turned into flexibility.

Leaders in those institutions kept communicating even when all the answers were not clear. That honesty built trust. Their consistency calmed teams. During crisis, communication is the oxygen of resilience. Silence drains morale faster than bad news.

Personal resilience requires boundaries as well. Hustle culture often glorifies exhaustion as commitment. In reality, exhaustion blurs vision and weakens judgment. The goal is not constant motion. The goal is a pace you can sustain over many years.

There was a season when my own schedule looked impressive from the outside. Twelve-hour days. Seven-day weeks. Travel, meetings, and calls. Results were strong. Peace was not. A health scare forced a change. I realized that rest was not an interruption of ambition. It was part of it.

Now I plan stillness with the same intent I plan work. Quiet time sharpens decisions. A rested mind sees openings that a tired mind cannot see. Leaders who guard their energy lead longer and better.

Resilience also grows through relationships. The idea of the self-sufficient leader is attractive and dangerous. Strong leaders still need people they can trust. Every major turning point in my career was linked to a conversation with someone who gave me perspective when my own view was narrow.

Isolation enlarges problems. A challenge that feels overwhelming alone often shrinks when shared with the right person. Great leaders surround themselves with truth-tellers, not just admirers. Resilience multiplies in honest circles.

Over time, resilience matures into anticipation. You begin to expect turbulence and prepare yourself before it appears. This changes your posture. You stop treating every crisis as a surprise and start treating it as a test you have already trained for.

I once worked with a team preparing for a large merger. We rehearsed difficult scenarios in advance. We practiced how to respond if talks stalled, if leaks occurred, or if key people resisted. When real setbacks came, they did not panic. They responded almost calmly because they had faced those moments in practice. That is the difference between amateurs and professionals. Amateurs hope for smooth journeys. Professionals train for storms.

Resilience also carries moral weight. The way you handle adversity teaches people around you how to act under strain. When a manager panics, panic spreads. When a leader stands firm, calm spreads. One person's steadiness can settle an entire department.

I often met CEOs who underestimated their emotional influence. They watched only financial numbers and ignored emotional signals. A rushed tone in a call, a harsh email sent late at night, a visible loss of temper in a meeting. These small actions could unsettle hundreds of people. Teams mirror the emotional weather of leadership.

That realization changed how I communicated when things were hard. I learned to speak more slowly, to project measured confidence, and to admit challenges without dramatizing them. People draw strength from tone before they analyze content.

Resilience does not remove pain. It gives pain purpose. Pain without purpose feels like chaos. Pain with perspective becomes character. Leaders who understand that do not waste their hard seasons. They turn them into depth.

Organizations can build this kind of resilience into their culture. It begins with what they praise and what they punish. When you reward learning and recovery, not just perfect outcomes, people experiment and grow. When you treat mistakes as data instead of disasters, innovation survives. The most effective companies I have seen are not the ones that never fail. They are the ones that refuse to waste failure.

On a personal level, resilience matures when your values hold you steadier than your circumstances. Purpose outlasts emotion. When your identity is anchored in a mission that matters, no temporary loss has the final word.

Hustle taught me how to move. Hard seasons taught me when to pause. Each setback became practice for future calm. Each disappointment refined my focus. Over time, the conditions that once shook me most became the very training that kept me steady.

In the world we now live and work in, volatility is constant. Crises arrive in cycles. Recovery time is shorter. Leadership in this environment demands more than intelligence or charm. It demands an inner steadiness that does not collapse when the outside world shakes.

When the storm passes, the people still standing are not always the smartest or the most gifted. They are the ones who stayed stable.

That is the essence of resilience. And it leads directly to the next idea. Leadership is no longer optional, and the call to step up cannot be delayed.

The Imperative

The future will not slow down for anyone. Every leader will live inside constant renegotiation with employees, regulators, customers, communities, and even the algorithms that now influence how people choose. Any trace of arrogance, heavy bureaucracy, or slow response will crack organizations from the inside. Agility, humility, and stamina will be the qualities that hold them together.

The pace of change has already shortened the life of every comfort. Markets shift faster. Technology moves from idea to impact in months, not decades. Public scrutiny is instant and unforgiving. Leadership can no longer be defined as holding things steady. It is the skill of moving with purpose when nothing around you stands still. Every decision is provisional, every agreement needs review, every win has an expiration date. The leaders who last will be those who evolve right in the middle of disruption, not after it.

My own journey prepared me for that reality long before I had the language for it. Every commission split, every unfair contract, every quick turn from one income stream to another taught me the same lesson. Negotiation is not an event. It is a way of operating. Hustle trained me to protect value. Trust taught me that the relationship behind the deal matters even more than the contract itself.

That truth has not changed. Negotiation is not a department in a building. It is a discipline in a person. It shapes the tone of every conversation that keeps progress alive. It shows up when you realign a team around a new vision, when you sit across from a regulator who demands change, when you talk with a community that wants proof of impact, not slogans. The ability to reach alignment is what separates leaders who keep momentum from leaders who watch it fade.

If you cannot negotiate, you cannot sustain leadership. Complacency is not negotiation. Pushing everything into process is not negotiation. Arrogance is not negotiation. Delay is not negotiation. Even polished words mean nothing when your body language, your decisions, and your speed contradict what you say.

Leadership is persuasion repeated with consistency. People do not follow titles for long. They follow alignment they can feel. When your message is clear, your posture agrees with it, and your pace matches the urgency of the moment, you earn credibility before anyone reads your résumé. That is alignment in motion.

At the same time, value cannot become an idol. You protect value because neglect invites erosion. You preserve trust because no budget can repair a destroyed reputation. You adapt quickly because relevance can vanish without announcement. These three attitudes form a simple test for any leader. Protect what matters, guard the trust behind it, and move fast enough to remain useful.

The next generation of leaders, in companies and across America, will not simply manage organizations. They will have to negotiate realities. They will stand between generations that think differently, between cultures that see power differently, and between technologies that change faster than policy can react. Their success will depend less on their ability to control people and more on their ability to connect people.

The warning is clear. Comfort is the new anchor. If you allow comfort to harden into habit, you will respond too late. Speak truth before silence becomes the unofficial policy. Adjust course before irrelevance becomes your identity.

Hustle taught me to move. Trust taught me to move with grace. Put together, they formed readiness. Readiness is not a mood. It is a habit formed by repeated decisions to act when others wait.

Every bridge you burn in a moment of ego or neglect is a road you will need later.

Mentorship Multiplies Leadership

Leadership rarely begins with a corner office or a promotion email. It usually starts on an ordinary day when responsibility arrives before you feel prepared. That was my story. I was still scrambling to pay tuition, still writing lecture notes on scraps of paper, still wondering if I could afford the next semester. Yet classmates kept coming.

"Explain this concept."
"Show me how to prepare for the exam."
"Help me understand this topic."

At first I said yes because I needed the income. Then I noticed something. Every time I taught someone else, I understood the material more clearly myself. Hustle kept me in school. Teaching began to make me a leader.

Mentorship is not a friendly talk over coffee. It is the deliberate act of building capacity in another person so that they can think, decide, and lead without you. It does not create followers. It multiplies leaders. Done well, it sharpens the mentor, stretches the mentee, and strengthens the entire team. Done poorly, it wastes time, creates dependency, and leaves the real gaps untouched.

Many organizations in America confuse the two. One company treats mentorship as a program. Names are matched on a chart, a quarterly chat is scheduled, and a report is filed that says "development completed." Another company treats mentorship as a responsibility. Real decisions are handed to younger leaders while a senior leader stands close enough to guide and far enough to let them think. One approach loses people. The other produces a pipeline.

You can see the difference in how time is used. A weak mentor spends an hour each month "checking in," speaking in vague encouragements and friendly stories. A strong mentor spends an hour each week helping a deputy make a real call on a client, a budget, or a hiring choice where the risk is manageable and the learning is immediate. When opportunity appears, only one of those deputies is ready.

You can also hear the difference. Weak mentorship sounds like, "If you need anything, let me know." Strong mentorship sounds like, "You take the first pass on this decision. I will review your reasoning at four o'clock, and tomorrow you will present it." One builds comfort. The other builds competence.

The results show up in outcomes you can count. Where mentorship is shallow, turnover is high, projects freeze when one person leaves, and customers feel the instability. Where mentorship is real, knowledge moves instead of getting stuck, continuity survives transitions, and performance continues even when key people step away. The scoreboard is simple: contracts renewed, audits passed, clients retained, teams that do not panic when someone exits.

The hidden cost of neglect is severe. A bright manager is hired with excitement and left alone to figure things out. Within a year, they leave. Replacing them may cost twice the salary. The bigger cost is the team that remains behind. They feel abandoned, skeptical, and slower to trust the next leader. Repeat that pattern across a division and you can feel the system grind. Bids are missed because no one knows how to price them. Clients move on because handoffs fail. Regulators lose patience because institutional memory walked out the door.

This is why programs that look impressive in slides can be more damaging than doing nothing. A "buddy system" that never transfers real responsibility is theater. Quarterly meetings with no follow-through are theater. Sessions where a mentor speaks and a mentee quietly nods are theater. These activities create the feeling of investment while leaving people unprepared. The letdown that follows does more harm than silence ever could.

Real mentorship looks very different. It is steady, not occasional. It moves from explanation to application. It begins with the mentor modeling sound judgment, continues with the mentee taking controlled risks on decisions that can be corrected, and ends with the mentee owning outcomes. The measure is not the number of meetings completed. The measure is the number of people who can now run the work without you. That is when mentorship turns into multiplication.

You can picture it as a simple weekly sequence. Early in the week, teach a principle. Midweek, assign a decision that uses it. At the end of the week, review what happened, extract lessons, and widen the scope slightly. No fanfare. No slogans. Just repeated transfer of knowledge, judgment, and confidence. When the person you trained starts training someone else, leadership has started to spread.

This is not only a corporate issue. It is national. A country advances when leaders rise and pull others with them. It stalls when people climb alone. You can watch it play out every day. A public agency loses three senior experts to retirement and critical projects freeze because no one taught the next group how to navigate the system. A fast-growing tech company promotes brilliant individual contributors into management and then wonders why teams fracture. A family business flourishes under a founder and then stumbles when that founder steps back, not because talent disappeared but because wisdom was never transferred. In each story, the cause is the same. Knowledge stayed stuck.

The stakes are rising. As artificial intelligence and automation take over routine tasks, what remains are decisions that carry real tension and real consequence. Machines can present options. They cannot carry the weight of judgment when values clash and time is short. That is where mentorship proves its worth. It prepares people to think clearly when they are tired, to stay steady when stakes are high, and to guide others in the middle of uncertainty. If mentorship in your organization only explains today's process, you are already behind tomorrow's demand.

There is also a personal memory that almost everyone shares. Think back to your first week in a new role with no guide. You walked in eager and walked out each day smaller. You did not know who to ask. You were afraid to admit what you did not understand. You went home wondering if you belonged. Now remember the person who pulled you aside, showed you where the real problems were, and gave you a choice to make with a safety net. One conversation and you walked taller.

Leaders create one of those two experiences every single day. They either shrink people or strengthen them. There is no neutral impact.

So what should change on Monday morning. Treat mentorship as a core duty, not an extra if time allows. Put it on the scorecard. Ask every manager, "Who can run your work if you are absent. What decisions did they own this week. What did you coach." Move from talk about development to actual transfers of responsibility with real feedback. Keep at it until the person you trained is training someone else. That is when leadership stops being a box on an organization chart and becomes a force that moves through a company and a country.

This is how gaps close. Hustle prepares you. Trust confirms you. Mentorship multiplies you. Leaders who invest in other leaders leave organizations that keep winning long after they exit. Leaders who refuse to invest leave fragility behind, teams that wait instead of act, knowledge that disappears the moment they walk out.

I learned this long before any title appeared beside my name. I had no office, no library shelf of my own, just pockets full of folded notes and classmates asking for help. I started because I needed to pay a fee. I continued because I saw what it did for them and for me. Teaching someone else forces clarity. It disciplines your thinking. It turns private competence into shared capability. Multiply that across a department, a company, a city, and eventually a nation, and you convert scattered talent into a living pipeline of leaders.

Teach someone today. Give them a real decision tomorrow. Review it, refine it, and widen their responsibility next week. If you do not, leadership stops at your desk. If you do, leadership outlives you.

The Handshake That Never Came

I still remember that office. The desk was wide and polished. The chairs were heavy leather. It was the kind of room where choices moved billions. I walked in with steady confidence. My suit was pressed. My shoes were clean. My name already carried some weight in the industry. The executive seated across from me was the number three leader in one of the largest banks in the country. A meeting like that could have opened many doors.

"Good morning, sir," I said, and extended my hand.

He looked straight at me, said nothing, and kept speaking to his assistant. His hands did not move.

I left my hand there. Ten seconds. Thirty seconds. Nearly two minutes. My arm began to ache, but I did not pull it back. In that moment I took inventory. My hand was clean. My clothes were in order. My shoes had no holes. Nothing about me was unacceptable. That silent refusal was not about my worth. It was about his choice.

Eventually, I lowered my hand and sat down. He asked a few surface questions, glanced over the proposal, and ended the conversation. The deal had no life.

When I stepped outside into the sunlight, something important happened. I did not feel crushed. I did not feel humiliated. I felt settled. I walked away with something more valuable than the signature I had gone in to win. I carried a clear decision about how I would respond to treatment I could not control. Rejection, I realized, is not the final chapter. It is the exam that determines who keeps writing.

In that pause, I made a private agreement with myself. If the handshake never comes, I will still give my best work. If the applause is withheld, I will not lower my standards. I will walk into every room as if it is my own championship game, whether anyone cheers or not.

Of course, my thoughts pushed back. What if he does not respect you. What if this proves you do not belong at this level. The answer that rose inside me was simple. Respect is not issued in one office. It is built over a lifetime of consistent effort. One act of dismissal cannot cancel genuine readiness.

That unanswered handshake became a mirror. It forced a choice that every professional eventually faces. Some people shrink when they are dismissed. They accept another person's behavior as a verdict on their value and quietly remove themselves from the track they once believed in. Others swing to the opposite extreme. They chase approval, lower their price, explain themselves endlessly, and allow someone else's acceptance to become their oxygen. They may gain short-term access, but they mortgage their future.

Leaders take a different road. They do not shrink and they do not beg. They stand with dignity. They let rejection harden their resolve instead of their heart.

This is where many systems in our culture fail. We have built environments that celebrate polish and overlook depth. We reward perfect answers in classrooms, but rarely teach students how to handle being ignored. We promote people who look impressive on paper, but do not measure how they behave when a door closes. We run leadership programs that train people to present well when the spotlight is on, but we rarely equip them for the quiet moments when the room grows cold.

That is one reason the leadership pipeline in America leaks. The problem is not a shortage of talent. The problem is a shortage of people who are ready to keep moving after they feel dismissed.

So the questions come back to you. When were you last overlooked or waved aside. How did you react. Did you shrink. Did you chase approval. Or did you remain steady. How different would your career look today if you had treated rejection as a test of your readiness instead of a verdict on your value.

The reality is direct. Rejection does not decide your worth. Your response to rejection shapes your future.

Over time I turned that insight into a simple habit. I began to handle rejection through three steps. First, I recognized it for what it was, feedback, not final failure. Second, I retained my dignity. No arguments, no pleading, no bitterness. Third, I refocused. I used the sting of that moment to sharpen my persistence and improve my approach for the next opportunity.

That simple pattern helped turn painful moments into useful lessons. Leadership readiness is not verified in one event. It is tested again and again until resilience becomes part of who you are. Falling down is not the problem. Staying down is. The person who stands up the eighth time after falling seven is someone others are willing to follow. That day in the bank office was only one episode, but in reality it was a rehearsal for many that would follow.

That experience reminded me of a different moment from history. In 1963, a young Bill Clinton shook John F. Kennedy's hand at Boys Nation and walked away with a clear vision. He believed that he, too, could one day become President. That handshake gave him a picture of his future.

I did not receive a handshake. My hand remained suspended in the air. Yet that absence gave me something just as powerful. It gave me fuel. Clinton drew energy from connection. I drew energy from rejection. Both encounters, although opposite in tone, created readiness.

If you want to test yourself, think of the rejection that still lingers in your mind. Write it down. Then write what it taught you. Often the lesson is worth more than the opportunity you thought you lost.

The handshake may never come. The applause may never arrive. The door may not open when you expect it to. The commitment still stands. Decide to be your own Super Bowl in every room. Decide that you will bring your best whether or not anyone is watching.

Rejection, handled well, does not discount your value. It proves it.

When Price Overshadows Value

The meeting began with promise. The head of Organizational Development at the bank had asked me to prepare a proposal for training employees in entrepreneurship. I poured myself into it, designing modules that blended structure with practicality—content that could spark new thinking, not just compliance.

She read it carefully. Her head nodded slightly as her eyes moved across the pages.

"Excellent content," she said at last. "Well-structured. Our employees need this."

Then she set the proposal down, leaned back, and let out a short laugh.

"But your fee is too high. I'd rather be the consultant making that money myself."

Her tone carried more than humor. It was meant to diminish.

In that moment, I had choices. I could cut the fee just to win the contract. I could take offense and walk out. Or I could do what experience had already taught me—protect the value of my work and maintain dignity.

"Ma'am," I replied calmly, "I always negotiate where structure allows. But I never compromise on value. This program is designed to deliver results. If the fee is your concern, perhaps the timing isn't right."

The conversation ended. I walked away without a deal.

It would have been easy to call it a loss. But leaving preserved something more important than revenue—it preserved credibility. And credibility is the currency that compounds when nothing else does.

***

Years later, my phone rang. A familiar voice introduced herself. It was the same woman—now head of HR, no longer at the bank, and facing a season with no income. She needed guidance on how to start and run a consulting firm.

I barely recognized her until she explained who she was.

By that time, my name opened doors across the industry. A single introduction from me could place someone into opportunity. The same person who once mocked my fee now reached out for direction.

That moment confirmed what I had already decided: never negotiate away your worth.

***

When price overshadows value, people often take one of three paths.

Some lower their standards instantly, believing acceptance is progress. But those who do become commodities—interchangeable, underpaid, and treated like items on a shelf.

Others walk away angry, convinced that pride is more important than partnership. They protect ego in the moment but burn bridges they may one day need.

Leaders choose a different path. They hold firm without arrogance, protect value without hostility, and walk away with composure when necessary. Over time, that steadiness earns respect even from those who once dismissed it.

The temptation to compromise never appears once; it returns at every negotiation, every skeptical glance, every sarcastic laugh. Each time you rise above it, your credibility strengthens.

***

This is where systems quietly fail us. Institutions teach people to seek approval instead of principle. Schools reward compliance. Corporations value likability. Leaders are encouraged to say "yes" quickly, not "no" wisely.

The result is a workforce that wins short-term access but loses long-term respect.

So turn the mirror toward yourself. Where have you undervalued your work just to gain acceptance? What would it look like to stand firm without arrogance? Who around you needs to understand your value again?

To act on this today, choose one area where you have undervalued yourself. Define the minimum you will no longer go below. Share it with someone who will hold you accountable. That single act strengthens leadership readiness.

The Value Guardrails

Know your baseline—where integrity and productivity stay intact.

Communicate outcomes—show results, not just rates.

Walk away with respect—because no deal is worth erasing your worth.

History reinforces the principle. Nelson Mandela spent twenty-seven years in prison. On several occasions, he was offered release if he would renounce his cause. He refused. He would not trade principle for convenience. That refusal earned global moral authority.

Principle is not stubbornness. It is identity.

Price may be negotiable, but value never is.

Hustle taught me to ask.

Trust taught me to wait.

Leadership taught me to hold the line.

Finding the Sweet Spot

Every leader eventually faces the test of balance—when to stand firm and when to adapt. Lean too far in either direction and leadership fractures. Bend too much and you lose respect. Push too hard and you lose relationships. The leaders who endure find the sweet spot: where principle stands firm and partnership stays alive.

At that time, my consulting firm's work came mostly from the private sector—banks, insurers, and corporates. The portfolio was strong, but expansion meant reaching further. I knew government work was the next frontier.

A conversation with a state commissioner confirmed it. He was warm, encouraging. Years later, he became governor and served with distinction. That interaction planted a seed: scale requires courage.

So I went bigger. I prepared a national-level program for a government department led by someone equivalent to a U.S. Cabinet Secretary. We had never met. I flew to the capital, walked into the department, and submitted my proposal.

To my surprise, the approval came within days.

But when I returned with new proposals, the tone changed. Resistance emerged. Negotiations dragged. The terms shifted. It became clear that if I pushed too hard, the relationship might break. If I compromised too much, my credibility would.

That was the moment to test balance. And I chose it—adjust structure, protect value. The decision opened the door to handle up to seventy percent of their training portfolio, with programs that broadened perspectives nationwide.

The lesson was clear: leaders who endure neither bulldoze nor bow. They bend without breaking.

***

The extremes are easy to recognize.

Hardliners may win arguments but lose allies.

Pleasers gain quick favor but collapse under pressure.

Balanced leaders build influence that outlives them.

This imbalance is visible across America's leadership systems. Schools teach people to obey, not to lead. Corporations reward compliance instead of courage. The result is predictable—a talent pipeline where people either become rigid bullies or agreeable passengers. Neither sustains a competitive nation.

What we need are adaptive leaders—people who can flex without losing identity and negotiate without losing integrity. Until this becomes a cultural norm, the leadership gap remains.

***

So ask yourself: where are you pushing too hard? Where are you giving too much? What adjustment would restore balance?

The Flexibility Matrix

Never bend: value, integrity, productivity.

Always bend: timing, structure, delivery.

Bend selectively: terms that create mutual benefit without eroding identity.

***

Colin Powell embodied this principle. He could blend firmness with diplomacy—bend enough to build coalitions, and stand firm enough to protect integrity. That balance earned global trust.

The sweet spot is not compromise. It is conviction with wisdom.

And those who master it become the leaders America needs—leaders who are ready.

***

The Salesman in the Corner Office

At the height of my firm's success, thirty people worked under me—researchers, trainers, administrators. That number was not about size; it was about responsibility. When people depend on you, leadership stops being a title. It becomes accountability measured on a calendar. Payroll does not wait. Obligations do not pause. Leadership is tested most when people depend on your decisions to feed their families.

That pressure clarified my real job. Although I owned the firm, I never used the title CEO. I chose Managing Partner. CEO signals authority. Managing Partner signals stewardship. It reminded me daily that leadership is not status—it is responsibility.

And that responsibility distilled into one discipline: sales.

Strategy mattered. Training mattered. Delivery mattered. But none of it sustained the firm unless I brought in revenue. Every time I walked into a boardroom, pitched a program, reframed an objection, or signed a contract, it wasn't just business—it was livelihood. Families relied on those signatures.

That is why sales is not optional in leadership. It is the law of reality.

Parents sell values.

Teachers sell curiosity.

Military officers sell courage.

Pastors sell belief.

Executives sell direction.

The question is never *whether* you are selling, but *what* you are selling.

When leaders sell fear, they create paralysis.

When they sell doubt, they drain energy.

When they sell confidence, they unlock action.

But persuasion depends on character. People buy because they trust the messenger as much as the message. Without integrity, persuasion becomes manipulation. With integrity, persuasion becomes leadership.

And persuasion starts within. Before you sell vision to your team, you must sell it to yourself. Before you persuade others to believe, you must persuade your own doubts. If you cannot convince yourself, no one else will believe you.

One strong leader can double or triple the output of a team. One hesitant leader can shrink it. This cause-and-effect chain is one reason America's leadership pipeline is thin. We raise smart managers, but not persuasive leaders. We reward oversight, not persuasion. And when the moment comes to sell vision, many freeze—not from lack of intelligence but from lack of readiness.

The Law of Persuasion

Your influence rises or falls in direct proportion to your ability to sell vision, trust, and value.

So let me ask you directly: if your title disappeared tomorrow, could you still sell your vision? Who must you sell to today—upward, downward, and outward?

History confirms the law. Steve Jobs sold desire for products people had never imagined. Henry Ford sold a way of life. Abraham Lincoln sold unity to a divided nation. Vince Lombardi sold belief to teams who became champions.

Every leader who changed the world first learned to sell what others could not yet see.

***

These four tests—rejection, value, negotiation, and responsibility—form the crucible of readiness.

- Rejection gave me persistence.
- Sarcasm tested my value.
- Negotiation taught me balance.
- Sales revealed my responsibility.

If I fall seven times, I will rise the eighth. Persistence remains the anchor of readiness.

Like Clinton's handshake with Kennedy, I have envisioned my own future. One day, I will serve this nation in its highest advisory capacity—perhaps as Chief of Staff or National Security Adviser to a President of the United States.

What began as a dream has become a vision. And visions, once timed, grow toward fulfillment.

Prepared by hustle.

Paid by trust.

Proven by readiness.

This is how we close America's talent gap.

This is leadership readiness.

ABOUT THE AUTHOR

Oluwabiyi Adeyemo is a management consultant and strategist with more than two decades of experience advising banks, insurers, regulators, government departments, and corporate leaders across West Africa, Europe, and the United States. Through the consulting firm he founded, he supported senior executives on product strategy, customer growth, human-capital development, institutional performance, and emerging domains in fintech and health technology.

After his consulting practice, he joined the Corporate and Investment Bank at JPMorgan in New York, providing payments product advisory and strategy support to corporate clients across North America and Latin America. His portfolio consisted exclusively of corporations with annual revenues above fifty billion dollars, reflecting the scale and consequence of the strategic decisions he supported.

He earned his first undergraduate degree in Finance, completed his MBA at the University of Roehampton in London, England, and later obtained a second undergraduate degree in Business and Technology from SUNY Delhi in New York, graduating summa cum laude. He is completing his doctoral degree in Strategic Management at Liberty University in Virginia.

He is the author of the Rural Equity Blueprint Series, which addresses advancing rural health equity, and the Rethinking Rural Governance Series within SozoRock's modernization and resilience program. His earlier publication, Shaping America's Future, examines leadership, policy, and national opportunity.

He contributes to data-driven health systems equity through The SozoRock Foundation, where he leads strategic initiatives, and guides digital strategy and health-access innovation at SozoRock Technology.

www.ingramcontent.com/pod-product-compliance
Lightning Source LLC
Chambersburg PA
CBHW070628030426
42337CB00020B/3953